Face to Face

Face to Face:

Meditations on Friendship and Hospitality

Steve Wilkins

Canon Press
MOSCOW • IDAHO

Steve Wilkins, *Face to Face: Meditations on Friendship and Hospitality*

© 2002 by Steve Wilkins
Published by Canon Press, P.O. Box 8729, Moscow, ID 83843
www.canonpress.org
800-488-2034

02 03 04 05 06 07 08   9 8 7 6 5 4 3 2 1

Cover design by Paige Atwood

Library of Congress Cataloging-in-Publication Data

Wilkins, Steve.
  Face to face : meditations on friendship and hospitality / by Steve Wilkins.
      p. cm.
Includes index.
  ISBN 1-59128-000-1 (pbk.)
  1. Friendship—Religious aspects—Christianity. 2. Hospitality—Religious aspects—Christianity. I. Title.
  BV4647.F7 W55 2002
  241'.6762—dc21
                                            2002007695

Contents

Face to Face:
Meditations on Friendship and Hospitality

So the LORD spoke to Moses face to face,
as a man speaks to his friend.

Exodus 33:11

Part One:

Friendship

Chapter 1
Its Necessity and Obligations

The clearest evidence that we live in a degenerate culture is the fact that we practice so little genuine biblical friendship; even the word *friend* itself has become a hollow term, drained of its biblical content and weight. This is precisely what we should expect as the influence of God's covenant wanes in a culture—the culture gradually becomes more brutal and more barbaric, and true friends become hard to find. In the fourth chapter of Ecclesiastes, Solomon laments for the oppressed, because they cry out and there is no one to comfort them. Here is a lonely barbarity, without comfort or companion. Contemporary culture is like those oppressed people, slaves to sin and having no friend to turn to. Society and community begin to die out, because sin isolates men from one another. Sin by its very nature is a proud, selfish insistence on going one's own way, and as such it cuts a man off from everyone around him. Whenever a society tolerates sin and covenant-breaking, loneliness becomes a common problem within that society, and its citizens begin to think of true friends as a luxury, not as a necessity.

This is the view which most people hold today, whether they have actually formulated the idea in their minds or not. They are not opposed to friendship, but they do not believe that it is an essential to their lives, especially when it is so difficult to make and keep a true friend. We are told from all sides, "You don't need friends. You need no one else beside yourself. You must be your own best friend. You cannot trust other people." Many people now live in this way; the solution to friendlessness is to pretend that you don't need friends at all. The folly of man has never been more plain: they encourage the very selfishness and self-centeredness that destroys true friendship, and then complain of loneliness. They never understand that the very thing they are focusing on—that is, themselves—prevents them from having true friends. As you can imagine, in a climate like this true friendship becomes nearly impossible.

Even God's people are not immune to this mentality. They fall into the trap of thinking that holy friendship, while it may be a nice thing to have, is really not possible. They have been disappointed in friendship so often that they have given up the hope of ever having true friends. But we simply must face up to the reality that disappointments in this area are to be expected. They are to be expected, first, because all men are sinners. No one is perfect, and an imperfect person will inevitably disappoint those around him from time to time. We should expect this even more as we consider the culture in which we have been reared. The nature of the world itself, the lack of community in our age, and the fact that we have been brought up in a world that is so barren of godly friendship, all mean that we are crippled to some degree in understanding what it means, what its demands are, and how to obtain it.

Of course, in a faithful covenant culture, children would learn these things without much formal teaching. They would learn them daily, living in a faithful society and family, constantly interacting with people of integrity. But when children grow up in a culture that is unfriendly—in the true sense of the word—they grow up without the skills they need to build and maintain biblical friendships and relationships. To a greater or lesser degree, this has been the experience of most of us. A few have grown up in very fine families where they have learned many of these skills and abilities, and know them almost instinctively. Unfortunately, most have not had this privilege.

Today, more and more people are growing up in abnormal families and hostile environments, and consequently do not understand the basics of friendship *at all*. Therefore we must seek to understand what the Bible teaches about this most basic subject, a subject that in other ages would have been frivolous to study. Two hundred years ago, it would have seemed a waste of sermon-time to preach entire messages on godly friendship, friendliness, and relationships. It is not a waste of time for the contemporary church. We must give this issue the careful thought it deserves.

The Grace of Friendship

Rather than implying that friends are a luxury, the Bible emphatically declares the opposite. Friends are not a luxury but an absolute necessity. They are not optional but vital. God, in His mercy, does not save us in isolation from other people, but rather in community with other people. If we are to be all that God commands us to be, we must realize that having godly relationships with friends is vital to the whole process.

This is more obvious to some than others. Those who have children recognize that they need to know these things and develop these skills. But the obligation does not stop with childhood or youth. It is essential for all of us who are still living, whether we are in middle age or old age. Although we may have learned these skills already, the importance of godly friends and godly relationships, and the duties and obligations they involve, remain with us as long as we live.

We can even say, with little qualification, that there is no possibility of living to the glory of God apart from godly companions. This is not to say that marriage, by itself, is a solution. It is possible to live to the glory of God and be single. The point is that whether you are single or married you must have godly companions, if you are to live to the glory of God. One of the most important and ignored aspects of courtship is the skill of being a faithful friend. If you would find a godly wife or husband, you must know how to be a biblical friend in the true sense of the word. If people spent as much time in being friendly as they do in picking out their clothes and fixing their faces, they would be far better off. Friendliness must be a focal point for the single Christian, man or woman.

Scripture says that God in grace places the solitary in families (Ps. 68:6). The meaning of this promise is not merely physical, although generally we, as individuals, do grow up in families, and move on to start families of our own. This is a true and glorious part of the promise, but it is not entirely, or perhaps even primarily, what God is speaking of in this context. He is talking about His grace. God comes to the rebel who has isolated himself in his rebellion (we are not *created* solitary), and God takes him up and puts him in a society, a family, and a community—the covenant family of the righteous. That is the principal meaning of the verse. The church, as the great covenant family, is the example of true community and thus is the pattern for all human communities in the world. It is also the example of the true family, from which all other families learn how to live. We learn how to live in our families by living within the Family of God and being taught by it. The church becomes the center of all society, because God founded church for that purpose—to teach and build up the people, so that we might live faithfully in all other areas of life.

For this reason I want to consider the nature and necessity of biblical friendship, and to do this we must ask a number of questions. Why must we have friends? What kind of friends ought we to have? What does it mean to be friendly? How is a friendship maintained and cultivated, and what will destroy a friendship?

Necessary By Creation

Humans are created as social beings, for they are created after the image of God. There is a wealth of knowledge in that single statement: "Let us make man in our image" (Gen. 1:26). God is not solitary; he is a triune personality. He is three as well as one, and the holy communion that is enjoyed by the three persons of the Trinity is the pattern for all earthly communion. We are so constituted by God as to live in the society of others. It is a nonnegotiable and undeniable attribute of humanity.

This was true of Adam prior to the fall. Adam was a perfect man created by the wisdom of God. He was everything that the infinite wisdom of God could make him. But God said, "It is not good that man should be alone" (Gen. 2:18). The man needed a companion; he needed someone who would be his friend. He could not live faithfully without a faithful companion. For this reason God created a woman, so that Adam would no longer be alone, and because of this God was able to pronounce mankind as "good." Adam would not be all that God intended him to be if he lived in isolation. He would not have been able to fully glorify God.

Thus the need for society is not something imposed on us because of our sinfulness and weakness. We are weak people, and weakness is one reason that we need friends, but it is not the first or most important reason. We were made for society from the very beginning. Specifically, human beings were made for the society of marriage. Unless a man has been given the gift of celibacy, it is not just a privilege to be married—it is a divine obligation. Men are commanded to seek a wife and should take it as seriously as any other command that God has given. They are to be active rather than passive in this regard because of their creation. Unless God has given him the gift of celibacy, so that he can be happy in the society of the church and the family of God without a companion, then it is not good for a man to be alone.

Our social behavior is something very natural and instinctive. This is why you feel uncomfortable if you ever run across one of those people who has no friends and does not care to have any, one who lives by himself and would rather not have anyone coming around. There is something wrong about this. Instinctively one feels that he is a suspicious character. He may be a fine man on his own, but the fact that he does not want to be near others or to develop intimate friendships indicates that there is something not right in his situation. In fact, while he remains in this state, he is not truly human.

We are finite beings and therefore cannot be self-sufficient. We are utterly dependent upon others, and the longer we live, the more we feel this fact. He is a fool who thinks he can live by himself. It is impossible. Nevertheless, many people are very attracted to the Romantic idea of escaping into the wilderness, living by themselves and not depending on anyone else. It is attractive because God alone is self-sufficient, and every rebel wants to be like Him. There is something in the heart of sinful man which dislikes being indebted to anyone. If a man is indebted, he is obligated to show his gratitude, and sinful man is not grateful. Instead, he wants everyone to be indebted to him. But God will humble and teach anyone who thinks in this way. He will teach him, one way or another, that he cannot be independent, and that God alone is self-sufficient. Every man is finite and thus cannot have within himself everything necessary for his own life and prosperity. No one has all gifts, talents, and abilities necessary to sustain his life. No one has all the knowledge necessary to live and exercise dominion.

One could raise what might be called the Robinson Crusoe objection. That character survived alone and prospered, didn't he? In fact, in the story, Robinson Crusoe was not really alone at all. He was indeed shipwrecked, but what did he do? He read books—he read the Bible. In this hard providence, Scripture was company enough. He also was not living on merely his own resources, as much of his survival and comfort depended on items salvaged from the ship, relics testifying to the society of his origin. He was not self-sufficient, nor did he ever profess to be. He relied on the grace of God, humbling himself under the mighty hand of God and was exalted in due time. He acknowledged his finiteness again and again and bewailed the loneliness and isolation which God had allotted to him.

Even if Crusoe could prosper on his own, what would become of his labor after his death? Nothing would come of it. Nothing would continue, for progress is impossible apart from mutual sharing. Ultimately, no man can reproduce himself. Man is not some sort of amoeba that can multiply by dividing. Man will die in isolation. The survival of the human race depends upon companionship, communion, and holy friendship.

Necessary By The Fall

Friendship is also necessary because of the reality of the fall. Each of us, by nature, has a fundamental flaw, a basic weakness, which we must acknowledge. Because of sin and not just finitude we desperately need others to help us—to watch over and care for us. Solomon states the case clearly: "Two are better than one" (Eccl. 4:9) because "If one falls he has someone to lift him up, but woe to the man who is alone when he falls" (Eccl. 4:10). He does not say "falls" carelessly. He is not speaking of a man tripping and falling down into a hole in the ground where no one can pull him out. He is talking about sin. Woe to the man who sins and has no one to help him. He continues in his self-righteous pride, and there is no one to say a word to lift him out of the pit of sin into which he has fallen. Woe to man who falls into sin. We need friends who will rebuke, correct, and admonish us when we fall.

In Hebrews, the writer warns the people of an evil heart of unbelief which was Israel's preeminent sin of old. He says, "Beware, brethren, lest there be in any of you an evil heart of unbelief, in departing from the living God" (Heb. 3:12). The apostle warns us to guard against unbelief, but what practical steps are we to take to do this? Will we keep ourselves safe by reading a certain book or attending a certain seminar? These things may be helpful, but the apostle himself provides the inspired remedy in the next verse: "Exhort one another daily, while it is called 'today,' lest any one of you be hardened through the deceitfulness of sin" (Heb. 3:13). We need the exhortations of other Christians to keep us from being hardened.

We hear this point again later in Hebrews: "Let us consider one another in order to stir up to love and good works" (Heb. 10:24). We need to be stirred up by others. We cannot live only under our own preaching; there are times when we need the words of others to provoke us to righteousness. And the very next verse adds: "Not forsaking the assembling of ourselves together" (Heb. 10:25). We are not to isolate ourselves. One of the chief problems of the church is that its members live by themselves. They do not interact with other people. No one rebukes them, because no one knows them well enough to predict how they will respond to it. When the members of a church fall into this error, the whole church is in danger. Thus we are commanded not to forsake assembling together. Each one of us must learn to be with God's people, so that we may know and have confidence in one another. Only then will we be able to give and receive exhortations against sin, and encourage each other toward godliness. Such knowledge and confidence is not optional, but necessary.

Exhortation does not always come from our own friendships. We also need the examples of others. The biographies of other saints are deeply encouraging because in them we see powerful instances of sinners being used graciously in the plan of God. The great biographies in the Scriptures—such as Hebrews chapter eleven—are in the Bible because God wants to remind us of these great examples, particularly that of our Savior in the gospels. This is why reading in addition to friendship is so important, whether we read the Bible or other histories. No one can be everywhere or see everything. No one can know everybody or be everybody's friend. So God in His mercy moves men to write about their friends, allowing us to get to know them as well. We need this.

Necessary By Grace

Friends are necessary because of the way that God dispenses His grace corporately. There will be no positive growth in grace apart from friends in covenant community. Of course, God does minister to us individually by His Spirit, and in that sense we are each the temple of God. God has ordained that His grace be dispensed through means. He normally works through the ministries of others in various ways, and thus when He saves us, He puts us in a place where we will receive that ministry from the covenant family. This relationship is defined by the church, and that is why we can say there is no salvation apart from the grace of God ministered through His people: the Word read and the Word preached by a faithful friend, the prayers of our friends on our behalf, and the gifts and the ministries of our friends to us.

In Ephesians 4:11–16, Paul writes that the elders are to teach and equip the members to minister to the whole body, so that the whole body might be built up. The worship of God in public is especially used by Him to build us up in grace, as David says in Psalm 122:1, "I was glad when they said unto me, 'Let us go to the house of the Lord.'" David enjoyed private worship and his own devotions, but he was especially glad to hear the call for the public assembly. He longed for the time when he could gather in the holy society of the redeemed.

The sacraments demonstrate this to us again and again. Baptism emphasizes the sovereign operation of God's Spirit as He initiates the divine friendship with God; the Lord's Supper reminds us that our Savior became man and offered Himself as a sacrifice for us. As He reminded His disciples the night before His death, He was doing it as their friend. He says, "There is no greater love than this, that a man lay down his life for his friends, and I call you friends." The Lord's Supper reminds us of this divine kinsman-redeemer—this divine friend—and even the elements of the Supper speak to us about the dependence that we have on God and upon our brethren. It is interesting that we use bread and wine rather than plucked wheat kernels and grapes. In order to have bread, we must take the thing that comes from God, the wheat that grows out of the ground, and then use the abilities that God has given us to grind the wheat, add the yeast and other ingredients, and it make it into a loaf of bread. Similarly, we must take the grapes, crush them, allow them to ferment, separate the liquid from the solid matter, and finally allow it to age to perfect its taste. It is no longer grape juice, but *wine*, and there is meaning in it. In this way God reminds us that, by his blessing and grace, men have had a hand in the making of the sacramental elements. Ultimately all blessing comes from God, but He uses human means to bring us to Himself and to nurture us in the grace and knowledge of Christ.

Everything around us confirms this. All of life points to the necessity of holy communion with godly friends, and everywhere we look, isolation equals death. Physically, man in isolation will die a physical death. Covenantally, the man who rejects godly companions will perish, cut off from the people of God. This message is repeated in the Scriptures again and again. In Proverbs 29:1, Solomon describes a man who evidently has friends but refuses to listen to them. They reprove and rebuke him for his own good, but he hardens his neck against them, and for this reason he is destroyed. Proverbs 18:1 states that "A man who isolates himself seeks his own desire, and rages against all wise judgment." The isolated man does not realize what he is doing, but he is in grave danger. Again, in Proverbs 13:20, "He that walks with wise men shall be wise, but the companion of fools will be destroyed." Without godly friends a man is destroyed.

Thus the ultimate fruition of sin—which is that ultimate expression of our selfishness, going our own way, and isolating ourselves—is the isolation of hell. Hell is described in the Bible as exactly that: it is the outer darkness where there is no communion, where you are left utterly and completely alone. This unimaginable punishment is horribly appropriate to wicked men who never wanted to listen and have holy communion with others. They rejected the covenant family. Thus God lets them go and allows them to live by themselves, with no communion with Him or with others, in torment for all eternity. It would be one degree of comfort to suffer with others, since at least there is some communion in that common suffering. But God says that hell is the place of no comfort at all. It is not the sort of place depicted in popular cartoons, where

Satan herds people a little room and plays tricks on them. It is a terrible place where former men and women are isolated in the most excruciating torment that can ever be imagined, alone for all eternity with no communion.

The loneliness of such a state only has force because we were not created to live alone. In the entire history of mankind, from our creation and fall through the gradual redemption of the world, the value of friends is constant. Godly friendship is absolute necessity because of our creation, the consequences of the fall, and the manner of God's dispensing of His grace.

Friendliness Before Friendship

First, what does it mean to be friendly to all men? Clearly the Bible teaches that we are to "love our neighbors as ourselves." Many times when the word "neighbor" is translated in the Bible, in the original language it is actually the same word for "friend." The term "neighbor" has a broad application: it may be your actual neighbor, your intimate friend, or, as the parable of the good Samaritan points out, it could be a complete stranger who has an urgent need. In other words, all men are our neighbors in the sense used in Scripture, and Jesus' parable teaches that we are obligated to be friendly to them, no matter how different they are from us. As an example, young people especially need to practice simply being friendly. Teenagers have difficulty acting friendly, often because they just do not know how. Sometimes it is because they are prideful, wanting to make fun of or humiliate others, so that they can feel superior to them. Teenagers need to learn that this is not the way to live in the real world. It may be a good way to get one's teeth knocked out later in life, but it's not a good way to live happily with other people. It may be a good way to be lonely later in life, but it is not a good way to profit from others and be profitable to them.

This general friendliness will express itself in two ways. We are first to be charitable to those with legitimate needs. We labor so that we will have the means with which to give to others. Paul says in Ephesians 4:28, "Let him who stole steal no longer, but rather let him work with his hands, that he may have wherewith to give to those who are in need." We labor not merely to supply our own needs, but to obtain an abundance so that we may have more to give. We should not want a salary increase to spend more for ourselves; rather, the rich man ought to see riches as a blessing because the more he has, the more he has to give, to show the grace and generosity of God to others. That is why we ought to desire success in our labors, and why we should work for more than what we need: because there are other people who have needs. God prospers our labors and blesses our efforts for this very reason. Paul says to the Corinthians that they have been given an abundance to supply the needs of their brethren so that there may be an equality (2 Cor. 8:13–15). He is not talking about socialism and the compulsory redistribution of wealth; he is talking about the purposes of God in giving some men more than others. He says that this equality, which comes when an abundance of one group supplies the need of another, displays the righteous caring of the people of God for each other. Our differences in social and economic blessings are given so that we may show righteousness in charitable friendship.

Conversely, it is a great sin to despise the legitimate needs of others when it is in our power to help them. Proverbs 14:21 makes it very plain: "He who despises his neighbor sins, but he who has mercy on the poor, happy is he." Again, in Proverbs 28:27: "He who gives to the poor will not lack, but he who hides his eyes will have many curses." The man who is ungenerous will regret the day he withheld his aid from others; it is not only a positive blessing to help the poor; it is a positive curse not to do so. There is a certain poetic justice in this. "Whoever shuts his ears to the cry of the poor will also cry himself and not be heard" (Prov. 21:13).

It is not necessary to pursue this subject at length, since any student of the Bible knows that mercy and generosity are major themes of Scripture from beginning to end. However, the command to generosity is also qualified throughout the Bible. We are clearly not obligated to meet all the needs of everyone around us. Our charity is to be limited in at least three ways: by our time, by our resources, by God's commandments—for example, "he who will not work, neither let him eat." There are people with real needs, whom we are not to help, because of their disobedience, until they repent. Depending on the nature of the request we may not be able to fulfill all that is requested of us; we cannot act contrary to one part of God's Word on the pretense of obeying another part of it. For example, there are many instances where one should not co-sign on another man's loan, merely because he thinks it is a need that I can meet; Proverbs is full of warnings about becoming surety for someone else in this way.

We are obligated to do what God says as far as our ability and resources allow. The needs of the brethren should always come first, before the needs of the world in general. Paul says in Galatians 6:10, "Do good unto all but especially those who are of the household of faith." We must first meet the needs of our own, and that may mean that there is nothing left for those outside—one of the consequences of rebellion is to be left without guarantee of support from the church. However, our charity is only limited by God's providence and by His commandments, and thus we must be ready to give what we can to meet legitimate needs, first those of our family, and afterward those of the world. It is a holy obligation to be generous, and it is a most hateful thing to see God's people without charity. We of all people ought to be generous, and we show it as a testimony to the world.

Meeting needs around us is only one aspect of our love toward all men. Love also means living lawfully toward our neighbors. Paul clarifies what it means to love both our neighbors and our enemies. It means keeping God's law. Love is the keeping and fulfilling of the law (Rom. 13:8–10). To keep the commandments toward them, to not sin against them, to do them good and not evil: that is what it means to love. Proverbs 3:29 says, "Don't devise evil against your neighbor" and tells us not to withhold what we owe to our neighbor when we have the ability to repay it. We are not to slander our neighbor (Prov. 24:28). We are not to tempt them into any kind of sin. We do good to them and not evil. Even if they sin against us, we still seek to do them good. A Christian cannot retaliate in a sinful way against his enemies. He may rebuke them or publicly oppose them, but he may not sin against them. We are under holy obligation to be friendly to all men. It is the first demand of biblical friendship.

Friendship Beyond Friendliness

A second demand qualifies the demand of friendliness: though we are to be friendly to all we cannot be the friends, companions, or intimates of all. Though we are required to be friendly, we are to have certain criteria for those we choose to allow into our intimate circle. Choosing close companions must be done very carefully. David, in Psalm 119:63, summarizes these criteria: "I am a companion of all those who fear You and of those who keep Your precepts." David does not just embrace anyone off of the street as his friend. He associates closely only with those who fear God and keep His commandments. He may show love and friendliness to an unbelieving man, but that man could never be his friend. Was David then simply acting like a snob, acting "holier than thou"? Certainly not. He recognizes the realities of his nature and the realities of God's demands upon him. "He that walks with wise men will be wise, but the companion of fools will suffer" (Prov. 13:20). According to David, you cannot have fools for friends and escape the consequences. No one could ever be so upright and holy that he could afford to have foolish friends because we are all influenced deeply by the people close to us.

Young people especially need to understand and avoid this temptation, as they are more susceptible to surrounding influences, whether they realize it or not. Their friends will either provoke them to holiness or encourage them in wickedness—it will be one or the other. It is never neutral. God has so constituted us that we will become like our friends. It is folly for a young person to think that he will be the one who will turn around all of his foolish friends. There are far too many examples in Scripture against this kind of thinking for anyone to seriously believe it, but still, being sinners, we always like to make ourselves out as great heroes who will save everyone else in the end. The reality is we are not great heroes, especially when we are young. And he will be another fool who fancies that he will be the exception. He tells himself that while everybody else is corrupted by bad friends, he will change them. He seems to ignore the fact that God has told him exactly the opposite. Over and over He repeatedly warns against ungodly companions. "My son, do not walk in the way with them; keep your foot from their paths" (Prov. 1:15). "Do not enter the path of the wicked, and do not walk in the way of evil; avoid it, do not travel on it, turn away from it and pass on" (Prov. 4:14–15). It is not merely advice; it is a command from God. You may not continually associate with evil men as friends, companions, or intimates; instead, you have an obligation to avoid them. The same warning applies to the evil woman: "Remove your way far from her, and do not go near the door of her house" (Prov. 5:8). "Make no friendship with an angry man, and with a furious man do not go, lest you learn his ways and set a snare for your soul" (Prov. 22:24–25). "Do not be envious of evil men nor desire to be with them" (Prov. 24:1). Paul summarizes the whole matter in 1 Corinthians 15:33. "Do not be deceived," he begins, because he knows that people love to think in this way. "Do not be deceived: evil company corrupts good habits." That is the rule; don't think you will be the exception. Don't be deceived and think that you're some great spiritual giant who will stomp all the little rebel pygmies in your way, and make them all faithful, submissive Christians. Evil company always corrupts good manners. Thus God prohibits a binding relationship with unbelievers, in situations that might compel a believer to perform ungodly practices, where he might be forced to do something contrary to God's Word. We are forbidden to do that: we may not marry an unbeliever, or enter into any relationship that might bind us to do ungodly things.

Characteristic Companions

These teachings have a broader application than just to our physical companions. We may readily apply them against watching television in an unguarded or inordinate way. To watch the many evil entertainments which saturate our televisions is to keep company with evil men. How is it that we believe we can watch these blasphemous comedies, these foolish sitcoms, these wicked dramas, and still somehow remain innocent and undefiled? Merely because one's evil companions are coming through an electronic tube and are not physically present in the house, does not make them impotent; if anything, it makes them more dangerous. They have a more profound influence than anyone realizes. The TV is a way for evil to corrupt good manners. It is a folly to think that we can prosper spiritually when we spend the vast majority of our time in the company of unbelievers. There was a time when it was easier to escape such company, but now the television has put them into every home. A man may live alone, never seeing another living human being, but he can still be corrupted by ungodly companions.

The child of God realizes these things, and he longs therefore for holy companionship. One of the first marks of a man's new heart is a gradual change of his friends. If they are not converted with him, he must eventually leave them behind. It may happen more rapidly with some than with others, but it always happens, for we always want to be with those who love the same things, who desire the same things, and who will teach, encourage and stir us up. For those who love God, God gives them a love for those who fear Him and desire to be holy; we have seen that David had such a love. Like him, we must avoid anything or anyone who hinders us in the progress of holiness and the fear of God.

We are known by our friends, because the qualities of our

friends reveal where our comforts, interests, and enjoyments truly lie. Men are naturally attracted to those with whom they agree: a drunkard will never be happy in the society of teetotalers. He will never be comfortable in the society of holy men who know how to drink in moderation. The former bore him; the latter convict him of his error. This example has a broader application, for the ungodly cannot tolerate the godly. "An unjust man is an abomination to the righteous, and he who is upright in the way is an abomination to the wicked" (Prov. 29:27). It is inevitable that the righteous man is as offensive to the wicked as the wicked are to the righteous. In light of this, each of us should pause and reflect on our own situation. What are your friends like? Whom do you desire to be with? Do you enjoy being with the people of God? Do you like to be with people who know more than you do, or do they bother you? Do you always like to be around those who are less intelligent than you are?

There is something wrong with the man who avoids those who know more than he; there is something wrong if he must always be the teacher and never the student. We should desire friends who know more than we do and who are farther along in their sanctification. If they will tolerate us, that is the kind of friend we seek. Of course, we should also have friends who are behind us, intellectually or spiritually. Relationships with superiors, inferiors, and equals are all necessary for true growth. Some people are saved later than others, some people grow up in a better ecclesiastical and familial environments than others, and therefore we are each obligated to help one another. Do you have friends who are willing to rebuke you when you sin or fall into slackness? Do you see the vital necessity of godly friends? Are you increasing in your friendliness? Are you actively building friendships among God's people? There will be no prosperity and grace if this is not so.

All of this, of course, reminds us of what a blessed thing it is to have a friend who sticks closer than a brother, our kinsman-redeemer, our holy Friend. Without Him as our friend, we would be of all men the most to be pitied. It is vitally important to have faithful companions, for He is the One who is preeminently the companion of His people. We need more of our brothers to live together with us in the same manner as our Savior: always with us, never leaving nor forsaking us, but causing us to grow in grace and faithfulness to Him.

Chapter 2
The Characteristics of a True Friend

God has designed us to need the fellowship and companionship of others. Prior to the fall, Adam was told that it was not good for him to be alone. He would not be all that he was created to be apart from holy companionship, and the same is true for us today. If Adam in his perfection could not remain alone, then certainly we, in our imperfection, should not attempt to do so. We need companions and good friends; godly friends are not merely a luxury, something nice to have if one can find them, but not essential for well-being. Rather, they are a necessity without which we will suffer. Isolation is not good, and complete isolation is not possible: every member of a congregation has inevitable associations within that group. These do not, however, automatically qualify as godly friendships. True friendship requires work.

The previous chapter considered the necessity of biblical friendship, as shown by at least three things: creation, fall, and grace. We are finite, social beings, whom God created to live together, and thus it is not good to be alone; we need someone to watch over us, help us, and hold us accountable to our faith; though God certainly does work directly upon us by His Spirit, He uses friends, instructors, and books to bring us to Himself and cause us to grow in the grace and knowledge of Christ Jesus.

I also considered two obligations of biblical friendship: be friendly to all, but not a friend to all. We are to be friendly to all men by living both *charitably* and *lawfully* toward others. We are to be charitable as we are able, and within the confines of God's Word, following the particular directives which He has given to direct and govern our charity, and wishing that our country would follow those rules as well. This is what it means to love your enemy, as Paul says in Romans chapter 13. Love means keeping the law. Though we are to be friendly to all, we cannot be the friend of all. It is impossible to have intimate friendships with anyone and everyone. Friends should be carefully chosen because they will either greatly assist or greatly hinder one's growth in grace. It is vital, then, that we chose our friends carefully, and this subject leads directly into our study for this chapter.

What should we look for in a friend? What are the characteristics of godly friends? The Bible makes it plain: there are two basic things that must be true of anyone who is to be your friend. According to the book of Proverbs, one's friends must be growing in wisdom, and they must be growing in holiness. It does not say that they must be the wisest or holiest people in the world. It does say that they must be growing in these two directions and able to encourage others in both. In the hard reality of life, no relationship is neutral. A friend will always be a help or a hindrance. By them you will either be advanced and stirred up in righteousness pleasing to God or hurt and hindered in your walk with Him.

Friends Growing In Wisdom

First, *a companion must be one who is increasing in wisdom*. Proverbs 13:20 again: "He who walks with wise men will be increased in wisdom," and those who do not walk with wise men will increase in folly. If I perceive that a man has no wisdom and does not seem to care about obtaining it, then he cannot be my companion. Proverbs 14:7 is also clear: "Go from the presence of a foolish man, when you do not perceive in him the lips of knowledge."

We are not to stay long in the company of a fool. We must be friendly to him, but we cannot be his friend because his ways are contagious. Avoiding a person's company like this must be done with good reason, and it requires some measure of wisdom to perceive wisdom in others. So how are we to know if someone is increasing in wisdom? What exactly should we look for? Such external, visible marks of wisdom do exist, and we must train ourselves to be aware of them.

First of all, we are looking for someone who has bowed the knee to Christ in repentance and faith—obviously the most basic attribute of a godly friend is that he is a Christian. He has ceased trying to be his own god and has acknowledged the wisdom of Christ and His righteousness as the foundation of life. The wise man has come to see his utter ignorance and his complete folly, has acknowledged that God alone is wise, and is ready to receive all knowledge and grace from Christ. Proverbs 21:30 states that "There is no wisdom or understanding or counsel against the Lord." If someone is speaking contrary to the Bible, then it is evident that whatever he is—and he may be many things—he is not wise. It doesn't matter how many bachelor degrees he has. Wisdom is not the same as cleverness and is not separable from ethical judgment. Anything contrary to the Word is folly and to be hated. Every true friend must be in submission to the wisdom of Christ and the authority of the Word.

Friends Love God's Word

Second, a good friend loves the Word of God because it is wisdom and delight. He knows that the Word is his life, and therefore precious to him. He does not occasionally dip into it as if it were a favorite novel; he loves it and feeds upon it and lives by it. The desires of David's heart in Psalm 119 are exemplary for the wise man. "I have rejoiced in the way of your testimonies as much as in all riches" (v. 14). David's sentiment is not a dispassionate appreciation. It is delight in the things of God. "I will delight myself in your statutes; I will not forget your word" (v. 16). "Your testimonies also are my delight and my chief counselors" (v. 24). "And I will delight myself in your commandments which I love" (v. 47). "The law of your mouth is better to me than thousands of shekels of gold and silver" (v. 72). "Let your tender mercies come to me that I may live for your law is my delight" (v. 77). "Unless your law had been my delight I would have perished in my afflictions" (v. 92). When afflictions come, unless one has a delight and a real love for God's Word, he will not be able to stand for long. "O how I love your law, it is my meditation all the day" (v. 97).

When a man is in love with a woman, his thoughts naturally dwell on her and move to her whenever his mind is free to wander. David loved the Scriptures even more deeply; his mind went to them constantly. "Your testimonies I have taken as a heritage forever, and they are the rejoicing of my heart" (v. 111). The Word of God is the richest inheritance one can receive, causing joy and affection in the heart of the heir. "I hate the double-minded but I love your law" (v. 113). "Therefore I love your commandments more than gold, yes than fine gold" (v. 127). "I rejoice at your word as one who finds great treasure" (v. 162). The Bible certainly doesn't denounce physical wealth and riches, and indeed often exalts them as a great blessing. But David rejoices over what he finds in the Scriptures as much he would over buried treasure. Of course a man will celebrate if he finds a treasure chest; but does he do the same for the great treasures in the Scriptures? David's love for the Word fills him and overflows into his verse; he cannot proclaim it often enough. "My soul keeps your testimonies; I love them exceedingly" (v. 167). We love the Word because it is the lovely wisdom of God.

This kind of love for the Word is not an abstract, intellectual approval; it should drive us to learn and know it better. The wise man is never satisfied that he knows it "well enough," but is constantly distressed over his own foolishness and ignorance. David, again in Psalm 119, is driven with this hunger and desire to know the Scriptures and to understand what God says to him: "Blessed are you, O Lord; teach me your statutes" (12). "Open my eyes that I may see wondrous things from your law. I am a stranger in the earth, do not hide your commandments from me" (v. 18–20). A stranger in a foreign town desperately needs directions. It is very troubling to be lost, not knowing where you are or how to reach your destination, and few people know this better than David—no matter where he wandered in the whole earth, he had this feeling constantly. There is no familiar place for a sinner. He needs God's Word to know how to navigate in the world, and if he does not have it, he is lost. Being lost creates a burning desire to know, and a longing to be found, and great thankfulness toward those who will share their knowledge of the way. David longs to be found again: "My soul breaks with longing for your judgments at all times" (v. 20). "Make me understand the way of your precepts so shall I meditate on your wondrous works" (v. 27). "Teach me, O Lord, the way of your statutes, and I shall keep it to the end. Give me understanding and I will keep your law. Indeed I will observe it with my whole heart" (vv. 34–35).

We should not desire to know the Word so that we can impress our friends with Bible trivia, or our teachers with an academic grasp of systematic truths. David wanted to know the Scriptures in order to obey them. "Teach me so I can obey" is his prayer. "You are good and do good. Teach me your statutes" (v. 68). "It is good for me that I have been afflicted that I may learn your statutes" (v. 71). Everything which instructs is good for us, even if it is affliction, tribulation and difficulty. We desire to learn by whatever means God has ordained. "Your hands have made me and fashioned me, give me understanding that I may learn your commandments" (v. 73). "Deal with your servant according to your mercy and teach me your statutes. I am your servant. Give me understanding that I may know your testimonies" (vv. 124–125). "Let my cry come before you O Lord, give me understanding according to your Word" (v. 169).

If you find a man who longs to know and obey the Scriptures, then you have found a wise man. If he does not know this, then it does not matter what else he may know. The chief book throughout all of life must be this Book. It does not matter how much history, biology, Greek, mathematics, or philosophy you know if you do not know this. It does not matter that you are an expert in any area of human knowledge. If you do not know this Book, you do not know what you need to know. David understood that there is nothing more important. So the wise man labors to understand the Word, to lay it up in his heart so he can follow it. He is not just seeking knowledge for its own sake. He is not just seeking knowledge so that he can feed his pride and impress others with it. He is seeking knowledge for the single purpose of being holy and pleasing in God's sight.

Wisdom Seeks Counsel

As one consequence of this, the wise man is not afraid to seek counsel from others. You may have noticed that the wisest people you know are the first ones to ask for help. It is the fool who always acts as though he needs no counsel, and he will not depend upon anyone outside of himself, unless he gets into very serious trouble. Not so with the wise, who always value other perspectives and lean on the wisdom of others, not trusting their own judgment to be sufficient. How many times have you been asked for counsel by someone who knows ten times more than you do? It can be rather embarrassing; you might think of saying, "You've forgotten more than I'll ever know. How can I ever give you advice?" You should rather recognize the wisdom and humility of such a request. The wise never consider it demeaning to ask for counsel, but the fool is ashamed to request advice from others and must be forced to do so. We would do well to memorize Proverbs 12:15: "The way of a fool is right in his own eyes, but he who heeds counsel is wise." The fool succeeds only in his own mind, but the wise man obtains wisdom by seeking it wherever it may be found.

Because the wise man is able to receive good counsel, he is also able to give it. By accepting wisdom over a long period of time, he has accumulated a store which may then benefit others. He does not merely parrot the opinions of the majority, or the experts, or what "they" say—whoever "they" are—but he can tell you what the Bible says and how it applies to a specific situation, and this kind of counsel is the most valuable, practical, and important that can be give. There is no success without it. Consider Proverbs 20:18: "Every purpose is established by counsel; by wise counsel wage war." In 15:22: "Without counsel, plans go awry, but in the multitude of counselors they are established." Beginning a project without seeking wise insight will almost invariably invite failure, because as individuals we simply don't see things as completely as we ought. "Where there is no counsel the people fall, but in the multitude of counselors there is safety" (Prov. 11:14). Again and again we must be told: there is safety in a multitude of counselors. This does not mean that all the counselors will agree, because realistically that is very seldom the case. It does mean is that God helps us to see His ways through the perspectives and counsel of others.

Therefore, a wise friend is valuable and even indispensable, for the wise counsel we obtain from him. And the more we are with him, the more we increase in wisdom and discernment. Remember the famous statement in Proverbs 27:17: "As iron sharpens iron, so a man sharpens the countenance of his friend." When we interact with our friends we sharpen each other's understanding, discernment, and insight into truths and situations. Have you ever felt that your sensibilities were dull and blunted, like a pencil that has been writing for six months and never been sharpened? Have you ever been enlivened, sharpened, and stirred up in love and zeal by holy conversations with others, who are excited and learning? Perhaps you have been sloshing along in the muck of spiritual and intellectual stagnation, when suddenly you have met someone who is growing in grace and joy, and he lifts you up. Without such friends it is easy to fall into a cycle of drudgery and laziness. When a man isolates himself, he begins to lose the edge in this thinking, the sharpness of his analysis, and everything becomes blunt and blurry for him. Wise friends and holy conversation are precious things because they save us from this sort of bondage. Proverbs 18:21 says, "Death and life are in the power of the tongue, and those who love it will eat its fruit." A person's friends, if they are growing in wisdom, will enliven him through their conversation.

Wisdom and Holiness

Increasing in wisdom is directly related to increasing in holiness. "He who loves purity of heart and has grace on his lips, the king will be his friend" (Prov. 22:11). To understand this saying properly, we must put ourselves briefly into the context of the ancient Near East, and try to think biblically and covenantally for a moment. In those times, the king was *the* man, the representative man, the exemplary man. The leader was supposed to be the best and brightest of all the people in the kingdom. The qualities of the king, then, were perceived as a standard for everyone to measure themselves against. What the king is and does is the model for what the people are and do. This proverb identifies the kind of man who is fit to be the king's friend, and thus not only should the citizen try to be acceptable as such a friend to the king, but he should also imitate the king in his standard for friends. The king's friends are those who love purity and holiness of heart, and who have grace on their lips, speaking wisdom and truth. Now what was true of the king's friends ought to be true of our friends as well. Biblical friends are to be those who are increasing both in wisdom and holiness.

This should go without saying because these two traits always go together. Wisdom and holiness cannot be separated. The fool is not holy and the wise man is not ungodly. No one is wise who is not holy; no one is truly holy if he is not wise. This may be self-evident in the Bible, but our contemporary culture has chosen to ignore it. For example, when considering a candidate for public office, it is common to hear supporters saying, "Don't think about his private life. We just need a capable man who has discernment and leadership ability. What he does in private is none of our business." Those of the world want to divorce wisdom and holiness because they do not want to be holy; they want intellectual absolutes without ethical absolutes. They say wisdom has no connection with a man's lifestyle when it has everything to do with it. If a man is not wise enough to depart from evil, he is not a good statesman or politician—he is a fool. If he cannot be faithful to his wife, or be a man of integrity, then he cannot know how to truly lead others.

Thus the one who is qualified to be our companion must have a burning desire to be holy inside and out. He loves purity of heart; he longs to be holy even when no one except God can see him, when there are no "church people" to observe and applaud his actions. He would pursue holiness if he were the only person on earth. He is circumspect in his walk, as Paul says in Ephesians 5:15: "He walks circumspectly, redeeming the time, knowing that the days are evil." He is not careless about continuing in the way of righteousness, but is able to think clearly, willing to receive admonition and exhortation. He flees even the appearance of evil, and he is concerned about his words: "Let no corrupt communication proceed out of your mouth" (Eph. 4:29). How we talk really does matter, much more so than we often think. We should speak things which are good for edification, imparting grace to the hearers. Recall that the king's friend has grace on his lips, so that his words edify rather than corrupt the hearers. He wants to avoid tempting anyone or undermining their godliness in any way. He is watchful over his heart attitudes and his thoughts; he longs to be pure inwardly. He watches against bitterness, envy, pride, unbelief, covetousness, selfishness, and all those other secret sins that bring dishonor to the God who hates all sin.

Snaring Souls

The one who guards against these things is an enemy to sin, and is the only kind of person who may be a true Christian friend. The one who is a friend to his own sin cannot be our friend. "Make no friendship with an angry man, and with a furious man do not go, lest you learn his ways and set a snare for your soul" (Prov. 22:24–25). A man who has no concern for righteousness, but who has an angry, bitter, resentful spirit, is someone we should flee from, because his friends will learn his ways. We must never presume that our influence is going to win out. Paul says, "Do not be deceived. Bad morals corrupt good intentions" (1 Cor. 15:33). Do not think as many young people, and sometimes their foolish parents, seem to think about their relationships. "It's all right for my girl to go out with that reprobate, because she might have some good influence on him." That is utter folly. *You will not* have any influence on them. Scripture expressly denies it. "Do not be deceived." Such people think more highly of themselves than they ought. They would do better to flee from sin. Sin is contagious, and we don't need much exposure to contract it.

A true friend will be a ferocious enemy to *your* sin as well as to his own. If he is not, he is able to do you much harm. The one who is a friend to our sin cannot be our friend. Those who flatter and condone ungodliness are not being friendly at all. Instead of a flatterer, we need someone who encourages, someone who loves us and speaks the plain truth to us, willing to give earnest encouragement if we are downcast, and faithful rebuke if we are in sin. He stirs others up by the example of his own godliness and integrity. His desire after Christ provokes others to desire His glory more.

Finding Good Friends

It should be clear by now that good friends are hard to find. What can we do to gain such wise and holy friends? I would suggest three paths to true Christian friendship. First, of course, you must make it a matter of daily and earnest prayer. Every good gift comes from God, including friends. Just as an unmarried man or woman should pray constantly for a faithful spouse, so also we should pray that we may find faithful friends.

Second, you should take advantage of the opportunities for

fellowship with other Christians, which requires attendance at a godly and faithful church. "Lone Ranger" Christians perish. Men who think they are sufficient unto themselves do not do very well. If they survive and make it to heaven, they get there barely, as it were, and with many scars along the way. The best place to find godly friends is in the household of God. The best place to find a faithful friend is in a faithful church. Of course, faithful church leaders insist that you come to the services of public worship on the Lord's Day, because of your obligation to God to honor and glorify Him— whether or not you receive from it anything for yourself. But thanks be to Him, we always receive something for ourselves when we seek to glorify Him, and in truth we get more from Him than He does from us.

In weekly worship, He has provided us a place to build good friendships, and we ought to receive this gift, by attending on such occasions to gather with godly people. We ought both to attend the service and stay there afterward. It is hard to make a good friend in the thirty seconds it takes to go from the back door of the church to your car. I 've talked with people who are in terrible situations, having no faithful fellowship near to them. They grieve because there is no one to understand and help them, and they have no chance of building an edifying relationship. These people would truly give everything that they own, to have what is available to many of us on a daily basis—solid Christian fellowship. Most of us do not even realize the blessedness of our own situations, but take it for granted and, in effect, despise it. Therefore take advantage of the opportunities that you have. Worship, prayer meetings, Bible studies, small groups, informal fellowship—take advantage of those things as you are able, remembering all those who long for the opportunities which you possess. Build biblical relationships with one another; make covenants to watch over each other.

Limits of Friendship

Even as we make more and more friends, we should remember that we are limited creatures. Christians often lack guidance and wisdom on this point. Everyone needs two or three good friends, but few can stand many more; frankly, we must admit that no one can possibly have the time for it. Do not try to be intimate and transparent with a hundred people. It is a foolish and unrealistic goal, and will accomplish nothing but to wear you out and set you up for a great and devastating disappointment. In a deep friendship there are a great many demands and difficulties which require time and work, and so most of us have time for only a few very close friends. Furthermore, no one is suited to be the intimate companion of every other Christian in the world. Certain qualities and differences in interest and disposition prevent some people from ever forming more than superficial attachment. Of course, we always strive to get along with every other believer, to live together in peace and harmony with them, and to truly love and esteem them by keeping the law toward them. But personalities are not interchangeable parts, and we are simply not able to be intimate with everyone. Be realistic in your goals, but be diligent in looking for a few good friends, with whom you can be intimate with confidence.

Not every friendship is on an equal footing, and this is perfectly natural and right. Not all friendships make equal demands on the people involved nor are they all equally intimate. To be more specific, we could distinguish three basic types of friendship. First, we have relationships with our superiors, that is, those people who are older and wiser than we are. Of course, they might be younger and wiser, but they are our superiors all the same; I know of men who are younger than I am, but who have far surpassed me in wisdom, understanding, grace, and holiness. In our relationships with these kinds of people, we are the primary receivers. We do not try to teach our superiors or voice all of our opinions in their presence, but rather we should learn from them, listening to their wisdom and asking them questions. Most of the demands in this friendship fall on the superior. He is the answerer, the giver, and the example.

We also have relationships with those who are younger, less mature in the faith, or less experienced than we are. Again, this could be someone who is physically older but who is a new believer or someone learning things which we have grown to know better than he has. In these relationships we are primarily the giver. In such a situation, one should not expect to receive as much as he gives, because his role in that relationship is to help the other to grow in the grace and knowledge of Christ. Being in this relationship we should be prepared to give in many ways: to answer questions, talk of edifying subjects, and above all, live before them as an example of godly faith.

Finally, we have relationships with our equals, that is, those who have nearly the same grace, maturity, and understanding as we do. In these situations there is a great deal of give and take, and we usually give about as much as we take. In a sense, each receives more than he gives because equals can effectively sharpen one another through interaction and debate. Between equals there is more opportunity for wholesome disagreement and even argument—not sinful, bitter, or divisive argument, but holy debate among peers that sharpens each one. We can say many things to equals which we could not say to one of our superiors. It would be brash and inappropriate to disagree harshly with a superior, because with them we ought to disagree carefully, discreetly and humbly. In the same way, it would be wrong to harshly correct an inferior, because we ought to teach them instead of bruising, embarrassing, or shaming them. With equals we are free to use the hard left hook and receive a right cross without much trouble, because we both know that we are both teaching and learning.

Obviously, we are normally more intimate with our equals than with those who are more mature or less mature, and we are more intimate with some equals than with others. This is a reality we should accept to avoid building unrealistic expectations. I find that many Christians do not think realistically about friends, and because they have such idealized expectations, they are disappointed in ninety percent of their relationships. Not only is it impossible to be intimate with a large number of people, it is wearisome and distasteful. It sounds nice in the abstract, but no human being can bear the reality of it. We simply do not have the capacity for such an undertaking: it would completely drain us emotionally, spiritually, mentally, and physically. Neither do we have the time for it. Intimates can make heavy demands on us, and we ought to respond by freely giving them our time and attention. Such generosity is impossible if there are too many of them.

Another reason to limit close friendships should be obvious: we are simply not equally compatible with everyone. This principle may not be very popular among Christians who are unbiblically idealistic about others, but it is a plain fact, commonly recognized as a reality of our nature, and it is not somehow more "spiritual" or godly to deny such created realities. By "not equally compatible" I do not mean sinful incompatibility, for clearly a cross, selfish, and proud person will not have a good relationship with anyone, and has no excuse for it. There are some people who have no friends because they are unfriendly, and who are lonely because, frankly, they deserve to be lonely. This kind of incompatibility can be solved by repentance and grace. But even apart from sin, there are elements in our makeup which cause us to fail to connect with some other people, and this is normal. Our personalities, interests, and tastes may lawfully differ, and such difference inhibits intimacy. We should always be concerned about possible sin in our relationships (or lack of relationships), but we should be equally concerned not to find sin where there is no sin. Though we each require intimate friends, it is entirely unnecessary and even unbiblical to be completely open and transparent to everyone.

We must learn to understand the various levels of friendships that we have with the brethren, and appreciate each of them for the benefits, privileges, and duties in each of them. We should not make equal demands upon every relationship, and should have the wisdom to discern each kind of relationship, and what we should expect to give and to get within it.

The Simple Truth

The third, and most important way to obtain good friends is simple: you must show yourself to be friendly. "A man who has friends must himself be friendly" (Prov. 18:24). I am amazed at how many people never get this into their heads and continually complain about not having any friends. We must devote ourselves to being the kind of people who are able to be worthwhile friends to others. This includes growing in wisdom, and studying God's Word and other good books to obtain such things as will profit others. We should intend to be holy in order to encourage others and thus give them a good reason to associate with us. No one wants to be close to an ungodly, halfhearted, complaining, and selfish person. Become the kind of person that is profitable to be around, for if you want godly friends you must be godly. Most people who complain about their loneliness fail to recognize that there is a good reason for it: they are wearisome, selfish, demanding, and self-centered; they have no wisdom to impart and no blessing to give; in short, they are burdensome people. It is quite easy to understand why nobody wants to be around them.

I've noticed that people will often try to take advantage of a visiting pastor because they think that he will act as an objective and sensitive figure who will sympathize with their problems and any perceived injustices against them. I once spoke to a woman who complained, "I don't have any friends, there are just so many cliques in this church. Nobody's friendly." She continued to whine and complain on this theme for some time. So I asked her, "Do you talk to other people like this?" She said, "Yes, but nobody sympathizes." I replied, "I don't blame them. It's no wonder you don't have any friends, as self-centered as you are. I wouldn't be your friend either." I felt that I had to say it like this and that she needed to hear it that way. I continued, "You are the one who is not friendly. Forget about yourself and be friendly to others; instead of complaining about how nobody loves you. Love somebody else besides yourself. And you will find that when you forget about yourself, other people will take interest in you."

The more you focus upon your own needs, your own responses, and your own treatment at the hands of others, the more unlikely it is that you will ever have friends. God does not bless such prideful self-centeredness, but He does bless—with the desires of his heart—the one who gives up himself to serve God and his neighbor. He has given us the blessings of wisdom and goodness in His word; if we reject those, why should He give us the blessing of friends which follows from them? If we are not serious about growing in wisdom and holiness in word and deed, we not only throw away any chance to have true friends, but what is worse, we will not have God Himself as our friend either. And it is better to live one's whole life and never have any companions except the One who "sticks closer than a brother" (Prov. 18:24). Better to have Him than to live with hundreds of worldly friends and not have Him. The most important thing in our lives is to be the friend of God, and this means caring about Him and seeking to glorify Him. The man who only wants to meet his own needs will never have God as his friend. But the man who forgets about himself and, in a sense, dies to himself, will have not only God, but many others, as his friends. Make it a matter of earnest prayer, and pursue it heartily in all godliness. Show yourself to be friendly, and both God and the brethren will be your friends.

Chapter 3
Cultivating Friendship:
Justice and Mercy

Our continual need for the ministry of faithful friends is inherent in creation. God did not intend us to live alone, for Scripture teaches that we are only truly fulfilled by having godly companions. These considerations started us on this brief study of biblical friendship, and so far we have identified two major points. First, we have seen the necessity of biblical friendship and the demands and requirements it places upon us. Second, we have seen two characteristics of a good friend: growth in wisdom and growth in holiness. In this chapter I will consider how to cultivate and maintain a biblical friendship. What are the ingredients of a profitable friendship that is honoring to God? How is it built up and strengthened? There are literally hundreds of specific points which could answer these questions, but I will focus, in this chapter and the next, on basic guidelines for cultivating friendships and then extending beyond those basics.

I think I can say with some authority and certainty that no friendship will prosper without the following commitments. I know they do not include everything that could possibly be said, but I am confident that they are at least the bare essentials.

Deal Justly With One Another

We must deal justly with one another. This is nothing other than the demand of love. In Romans 13:10, Paul gives a summary of love: "Love does no harm to a neighbor; therefore love is the fulfillment of the law." In our friendships we are to love. We are to love our neighbors, and this means, among other things, always doing them good and not evil. To cultivate biblical friendships with our brethren, we must deal with them in love, which means dealing justly and lawfully with them. There are several ways of dealing unlawfully and unjustly, which are barriers to friendships and must be avoided. The book of Proverbs is extremely helpful in identifying these, and I will focus there.

"Do not withhold good from those to whom it is due, when it is in the power of your hand to do so. Do not say to your neighbor, 'Go, and come back, and tomorrow I will give it,' when you have it with you" (Prov. 3:27–28). Here is a basic rule of friendship: do not withhold from someone what you owe to them. When you are able to repay, you have no right to withhold payment. You ought to be serious about repaying all debts, but give specially attention to those of your friends. Do not think that a friend will understand and ignore a debt simply because he is your friend; you have an obligation to love and deal justly with him, just as with anyone else. We must be meticulous about returning the things that we borrow (especially books!). This is a matter of basic integrity, but it is shocking how many friendships break up or drift apart, simply because those involved cannot trust one another. This is one symptom of the large and distressing problem of honesty in the Christian world today. Christian businessmen have often told me that they do not like dealing with other Christians, and I myself, working in a small business of my own, know why they have this complaint. Christians will sometimes call us, asking us to send them sermon tapes and promising that their check is in the mail. Six months and five notices later, I give it up and write it off—one more professing Christian who is a liar and a thief.

I know that we can sometimes unintentionally forget a debt, but forgetting is never an excuse. We need to be extremely conscientious about all borrowing. If you want to buy what belongs to another, make an offer, but do not steal it under the guise of borrowing it. How many things have you owned which other people—even "good Christian people"—have taken and never given back? They continue to use it, and they never offer to buy it. Often they forget that it is even borrowed. In fact, they have stolen it. "The wicked borrows and does not repay, but the righteous shows mercy and gives" (Ps. 37:21). It is a peculiar mark of the wicked man to borrow and not pay back. This is thievery, and all thieves will be cast into the lake of fire, no matter how great their profession or testimony is. In other words, learn to take this very seriously. There is far too much of this sort of theft in the circles of professing Christians, as some of us unfortunately know by experience. Be over-scrupulous about payment, especially in your business dealings. When you put a charge on your credit card, pay for it. If you put something on your tab, pay it. Do not make business owners curse your name and dread your approach because they know it is hard to get money out of you. Be absolutely honest in all your dealings, public and personal. If you want to have a profitable friendship, do not steal from one another.

Another way to deal justly with others is to make restitution. The Bible always demands restitution for damage to another's property, and in addition he ought to receive something more to make him better off than before. God requires this kind of twofold restitution in some cases, requiring the offender to restore both the item and the value of the item. If someone were to borrow a rare $3,000 vase and happen to break it, what should he do? If he cannot replace it directly, he ought to pay the owner $6,000 or $9,000, so that the owner can replace it and have something extra. As you can see, this sort of just dealing can get expensive. Why not simply replace the value of the vase only? Because additional restitution leaves no room for bitterness or regret. The owner of the vase will not afterward think of the offender as a careless person who cannot be trusted with anything. He will think of him as an honorable, careful person, because he voluntarily restored the broken item with interest, and because of what happened, the owner could now buy something of twice the quality. Any possible bitterness is completely short-circuited. It may be a sacrifice to your pocketbook, but the preservation of our neighbor's friendship is always more important than our money.

We can also deal unjustly in situations other than that of simple restitution, whenever in any way we take advantage of our friends to our own profit. We can rob our friends in very subtle ways. One is using the friendship as an excuse to not pay for their work. Whether the friend is a plumber, lawyer, doctor, contractor, or computer repairman, there is a particular temptation to call him first for minor problems or questions, and expect him to do it for free or at a reduced rate. Of course, friends enjoy giving to one another, and there is nothing wrong if a friend wants to volunteer his time for you. But do not presume upon his generosity and kindness, and expect his assistance simply because he is a friend. Every laborer is worthy of his hire, even if he is a close friend of yours. Presumption of generosity will quickly wear down any friendship.

The other side of this coin is equally important. There is nothing at all unfriendly about a friend who expects to be paid for his work. Sometimes Christians seem to become uncomfortable if other Christians, and especially Christian friends, want to be paid for their services to them. Such a feeling springs from a misunderstanding of friendship, business, and Christianity. Dealing justly means that we support and provide for one another in our occupations, giving fair recompense and giving without expecting to receive. Do not be offended by always expecting to receive. Do not have friends who dread your requests for help because they know that you take advantage of others who help you. Friendship will never grow without basic integrity and righteous dealing. It is a terrible thing to let a few dollars stand in the way of a friendship. Friendships are worth more than that. We should never presume upon anyone, and never fail to deal justly with one another.

Holy Sympathy and Compassion

If such aboveboard dealing is the foundation of friendship, a holy sympathy and compassion allows it to grow and deepen. This is part of what it means to bear one another's burdens, sympathizing with our friends in their joys and sorrows. "Rejoice with those who rejoice, and weep with those who weep" (Rom. 12:15). We are to join with our friends in their blessedness as well as in their afflictions. One of the peculiar comforts we have, by virtue of our Savior's priestly intercession for us, is that He is able to be touched with the feeling of our infirmities. He is not just a heavenly businessman who deals with us only on a professional basis. He feels with us in our struggles and he understands us. He is able to exercise holy sympathy even with His wicked, rebellious brethren. To exercise holy sympathy with a friend is one of the most profitable duties we can perform in a biblical friendship. Some of us particularly need to learn how to "rejoice with those who rejoice," especially when we ourselves may be unhappy or struggling with an affliction that is unknown to our friends. How should we respond when a friend has been blessed in some way, and he shares it with us? Do not reply gloomily, "Oh, I'm very happy for you." He feels obliged to ask, "What happened to you?" Then he has to listen to the long, sad tale because his friend cannot bear to see other people rejoice when he himself does not happen to feel like it. This kind of person will always to let others know that he is not as happy as they are, in order to bring them down into his gloom. His basic motto is "If I can't be happy, I won't let anyone else be happy either." Obviously, this is not a good way to make and keep friends. If he does not rejoice with those who rejoice, he should not be surprised when people do not rejoice with him at all. They would rather go to someone who enjoys and shares God's goodness with them. Friendship requires a holy sympathy for gladness.

Of course, we should also meet the particular necessities of our friends. True compassion is more than sympathetic feelings, for it expresses itself in action. True compassion drives us to meet the necessities of our brethren, as the good Samaritan did in Jesus' parable. Who was the true "friend" (the term translated "neighbor")? The friend was the one who actually helped the victim, who picked him up, bound his wounds, and paid for his recovery. The others may have felt his pain from a distance but they did not stop to help. Our Savior is not only called sympathetic but also merciful. He is one who is touched with the feelings of our infirmities and moved to take action and relieve them. True compassion always expresses itself in this way to relieve the necessities of others. It means, in effect, being willing to die to yourself for the sake of your friend. It means to weep with them even if you feel like rejoicing over your own blessings. It means rejoicing when them even if you feel like weeping over your own afflictions. In God's providence it is an opportunity to forget your cares and rejoice with him. Sympathy and compassion in all things will make you a more friendly person.

Proverbs 25:20 is wonderfully picturesque and appropriate for this point. "Like one who takes away a garment in cold weather, and like vinegar on soda, so is one who sings songs to a heavy heart." The simile of the proverb communicates its point in a memorable and perfectly clear way: "Don't demand frivolity in a time of grief." I am sure we have all known people who are continually trying to be funny and really do not know when to stop. There is a time to make jokes, and there is a time to refrain from joking. To take away a coat in winter—to rob someone of his only comfort and protection from a numbing grief—is harmful, cruel, and mean-spirited. Vinegar and soda, when mixed, react violently. It is not wise to put them together, and in the same way, thoughtless levity is not a comfort but a provocation. The one who is grieving is more likely to hit the jester than to laugh at him—and so poorly advised frivolity can easily turn ugly and hurt both parties involved.

It is far better to weep with those who weep and point them to the Savior for healing and comfort, rather than to try to raise their spirits artificially with untimely and inappropriate humor.

Consideration and Sensitivity

The third requirement for strong friendship is consideration and sensitivity, including common courtesies but also going above and beyond them. In America today we not only seem to lack basic politeness, we sometimes even mock those who do have them. I live in the South, and I know that southerners have a certain reputation elsewhere in the country for their courtesy. People tend to consider the courtesy excessive and try to make a joke out of it. Basic courtesy is the oil that helps us get along throughout every day. Not everyone is naturally as smooth as silk, and some people have some rough edges that can scrape and tear those around them if they are not careful. Training in basic courtesy puts some padding on their sharp edges so that they do not accidentally hurt others. That is the only way everyone can get along daily in the world. Now, as those in the world continue to break God's covenant—as the implications of their rebellion begin to develop and make them more calloused—we must especially guard against being dragged with them into that kind of insensitivity. All of us have found ourselves doing it at one time or another. "They" don't speak, so you don't speak. They are unkind and thoughtless, so you harden yourself too. They bump into you, make a rude comment, and keep going, and so do you. After living in such an environment, most people would soon start acting the same way. But we must not allow ourselves to become inconsiderate just because the world around us is. We must not allow ourselves to fall into that kind of thoughtless, callous hardness.

One way to be considerate to our friends is to avoid imposing on their kindness or hospitality. "Seldom set foot in your neighbor's house, lest he become weary of you and hate you" (Prov. 25:17). The formulation may be somewhat blunt, but it certainly gets the message across. Of course, it is a normal expression of friendship to be frequently together because friends enjoy being together. The point of the proverb is to avoid going overboard. Do not overburden your friend. Those whose insensitivity leads them to make unreasonable demands upon their friends cause unreasonable disruption. Again, there are happy disruptions about which we should avoid being overly sensitive as well as insensitive. Whenever I preach on issues like this I am always afraid that someone with a tender conscience will think I am rebuking them directly and will panic and never make an unexpected visit again. My point should not be taken in that way. All guests are disruptive to some extent, but there are unreasonable disruptions which interfere with the normal routine of the household and set stumbling blocks for between friends. Someone who is thoughtless for the welfare and comfort of his friend creates only contempt for himself. The old proverb is more true than not: "Fish and company both stink after three days." Do not constantly "mooch" off of your friends. A little mooching is understandable but overdoing it will certainly lose them. Do not presume upon the hospitality of each other. Even though it is good to be hospitable, and we each should pursue it wholeheartedly, do not take advantage of some else's kindness. Be thoughtful and considerate.

Loyalty and Faithfulness

The fourth thing that friendship demands is loyalty and faithfulness. "A friend loves at all times, and a brother is born for adversity" (Prov. 17:17). A good friend is one who sticks; he is always there and willing to give his love to others. This does not mean he is a yes-man who always agrees with his friends, nor does it mean he will always commiserate with them—sometimes he must rebuke them when they are sinning or feeling sorry for themselves. Whatever love demands, he is at all times willing to give. He is constant, not here today and gone tomorrow. He is like a brother, born to cling through adversity. The writer of Proverbs includes a number of warnings about fair-weather friends. "Wealth makes many friends, but the poor is separated from his friend" (Prov. 19:4). "Many entreat the favor of nobility, and every man is a friend to one who gives gifts" (19:6).

The poor man is abandoned even by his own family; how much more will his friends desert him? They do so because he is no profit or advantage to them. The rule of "networking" in the modern world is to make friends only with people who can help you and advance your interests. It is true that wealth attracts many friends, but they are only friends of wealth, not friends of a person. They love the gifts but not the giver. Then, if the wealth or fame happens to dry up, and they see that there is no longer any advantage to be gained, they jump ship. How many young college football players have proven this principle, ending up as lonely men because they thought people really loved them while they made touchdowns and headlines? The only thing their so-called "friends" loved was their own association with someone famous. Matthew Henry says of such people: "These are swallow friends. They leave when winter comes." Much of what passes as friendship in the world is simply thinly disguised self-interest; that is all it is, and all it ever will be.

A true friend loves at all times, concerned to constantly give and do good to his companions. Therefore, until the root of selfishness is sufficiently weakened by God's grace, true friendship, which includes loyalty and faithfulness, cannot grow. Loyalty is manifested by faithfulness, and faithfulness keeps its promises. Friends are often far too careless with their words and promises, failing to make appointments, promising to go somewhere when they never intend to go at all. That sort of thing is not friendly; it is manipulative. They make a show of caring by promising to attend an event, which is nothing more than a white lie told to save face. Friends ought to be completely dependable, even when they promise to their own hurt.

No friendship can prosper unless the truth is being spoken in love. It is not enough merely to speak the truth and assume we are loving. Considerate phrasing does not compromise a rebuke. Of course, sometimes we do have to say things that are unpleasant and painful. On rare occasions, we must be fairly brutal with our friends, telling them bluntly how things stand and effectively flattening them by it. But most of the time, you should say it so that they can receive it as easily as possible, sufficiently forceful to accomplish the point, but not verbal bulldozing. "Open rebuke is better than secret love. Faithful are the wounds of a friend, but the kisses of an enemy are deceitful" (Prov. 27: 5–6).

Some enemies will seem to be more friendly than true friends, but flattery of sin will always unmask them. It is hard to be a truthful and (if necessary) a wounding friend, but this is the test of true love. Some people might object that a brutally truthful person is not likely to have many friends. Perhaps this is true, but it need not be the case. Such a man *might* have few friends, but he can be certain that none of those he does have are hypocrites. If he truly and wisely speaks the truth in love, only hypocrites will not be able to stand him. Wise men will love him, and according to Proverbs that is the goal we ought to strive for. "Do not correct a scoffer, lest he hate you; rebuke a wise man, and he will love you" (Prov. 9:8). There will always be some people who believe themselves to be true and loving companions, when in fact their rebukes are self-centered, proud, ill advised, and offensive even to a wise man. But the wise will receive and appreciate a rebuke from the wise. "He who rebukes a man will find more favor afterward than he who flatters with the tongue" (Prov. 28:23). Notice that no one is guaranteed his remarks will garner favor at the moment he makes them, because we are all sinners and do not generally like to hear others say that we have done something wrong. But afterward, when things cool down, the true friend will have more favor than the man who flatters. The flatterer may be loved in this world, but he will certainly be cursed in the next. It is better to be a true friend today, even if your friend thinks of you as his enemy until tomorrow. Friendship never grows without loyalty and faithfulness.

What Kind of Friend Are You?

We have reviewed many qualities that make a good and lasting friend, and now we ought to seriously apply these principles to ourselves. Are you this kind of friend? Are you just? Are you compassionate, considerate, faithful and loyal? We are called to be all these things, and only by adopting these virtues will we be profitable friends to others. Do you not have friends? Be ready to acknowledge that you may not be a friendly person. Are you one who profits others by associating with them? Whether you rejoice or weep with them, comfort them or disturb their complacency, are you causing others to grow?

Do you make unreasonable demands upon others? If you are, do not be surprised that people do not want to be close to you. Do not assume that *their* selfishness is the cause; you are not the only other person in the world, and your friends have many demands from many different people. Do you always ask what others can give to you, or do you try to find out what you can give to them? Remember that the loneliest people are usually the most selfish people, and that if you want friends, you must prove yourself friendly. I guarantee that if you do this, you will have more people than you can handle clamoring to be your friend.

Do You Want a Real Friend?

The second application we should make is this: do you *want* the kind of friend I have described? It is not enough to merely "want friends." You must want a real friend, a friend who will love you, who will stamp out your sin, and who will tell you when you are wrong and encourage you when you are right. He will be an enemy to you sometimes; he will not flatter you, and he will tell you the truth even when you want to be flattered. Sadly, most people want sycophants for friends. Historically, a sycophant was a parasite in the court of a king who flattered him, and encouraged others to do the same, in return for royal favor. They always said what the king wanted to hear. Today, far too many people, thinking themselves little kings, want such sycophantic friends who will worship them, applaud everything that they say, never disagree with them, always respect them, and even quote them. He who believes he has a natural right to have followers like this is haughty and self-righteous, and will have considerable trouble finding anyone willing to play along. He doesn't need friends; he is already his own best friend.

We all need friends who love, esteem, and respect us, but who will never flatter us. We all need them, but do we yet want them? If we desire friends and companions, do we truly understand what it is we ask for? Most people do not; they might want a servant or a toady but they do not want a solid, earnest, biblical friend. You must decide whether you truly want friends. Would you be offended if someone actually sought to love you and do you good? If so, you are in the grip of sin already. Repent and turn away from yourself, your pride and your self-worship, so that you can love others and learn from Christ what it means to be a friend to sinners. For that is exactly what we are called to be. No one can find perfect people to befriend—people who never disappoint you or sin against you. A perfect friend would require very little sacrifice; anyone could be a friend to an angel. We are called to be friends to sinners. That path is a hard one, but the rewards are rich for those willing to exercise an abundance of grace, selflessness, and real, abiding love.

Chapter 4
Cultivating Friendships:
Love And Good Works

The man who would have friends must show himself friendly. This is not something that we innately know how to do, simply by being human. Certainly some Christians have been privileged to live in happy, sanctified homes, and grew up under parents who had the grace to understand these matters, who taught and trained them in the principles of friendship from their youth onward, within the home. These few know instinctively about the demands and joys of making and keeping friends, and cultivating deep and enduring friendships. But sadly, most of us have not had such an upbringing, and as our culture continues to disintegrate, fewer and fewer of our young people will experience it. People in our day are generally less wise in these basic matters than they were one hundred and fifty years ago.

If it is vital that we have godly friends, and the Bible says it is, then we must know how to cultivate such relationships with each other. The best place to find good friends is in the household of faith. The Scriptures teach us those things that are necessary to promote biblical friendships, regardless of the particular type of friendship or the particular degree of intimacy involved: we must deal justly, paying debts, giving restitution, and paying for services we receive; we must have holy sympathy and compassion; we must be considerate and sensitive; and we must be loyal and faithful, constant in each other's afflictions and speaking the truth in love. In the previous chapter we were concerned with cultivating the bare essentials of friendship. But we must go beyond these too.

Faithful Exhortation and Encouragement

Our friendships with one another should be patterned after God's friendship with us. According to the proverb, we all have a friend who "sticks closer than a brother"—a friend none other than the triune God, particularly the person of the Holy Spirit. In the upper room discourse recorded in John 14:16, Christ tells the disciples, "I will pray to the Father and He will give you another Helper, that He may abide with you forever." In John 16:7, He says, "Nevertheless, it is to your advantage that I go away, for if I do not go away the Helper will not come to you, but if I depart I will send Him to you." In each case Jesus is using the single Greek word *parakletos*, which is translated as "Comforter" in the King James and New American Standard, and as "Helper" in the New King James. Unfortunately, neither of those English words can successfully gather up all the meaning of the original Greek term. It is the noun form of a verb meaning to exhort, to comfort, or to encourage, and literally means "one who is called alongside." The *parakletos* is the one who comes beside us to uphold and help us.

From this, we might think of Him like a friend who will stand by and put an arm around us when we are grieving, comforting and sympathizing until we are ourselves again. Although this is a part of the Spirit's work, the idea is actually much broader. Comfort alone tends to mean only something we need when we are distressed, but the *parakletos* is also one who exhorts, giving to a man everything he needs to be strengthened and revitalized. Sometimes the Spirit will strengthen us by holding us gently, calming us, and sympathizing with us. Other times we need, figuratively speaking, a slap in the face and the spiritual equivalent of "Snap out of it!"

We occasionally need someone to make a fuss over us, to give us their attention and bandage our injuries, but more often we need a stiff rebuke and a strong opponent to drive out our rebellion. This is exactly how the Spirit deals with us as His friends. Whether He encourages, exhorts, or rebukes, He is always working to sanctify and strengthen us, and to make us a fit dwelling place for God. As we learn to be holy friends with each other, we must learn to imitate the work of the *parakletos* in our own relationships, comforting and exhorting one another in all gentleness, sternness, and holiness.

Consider now that fairly well-worn passage in Hebrews: "Let us consider one another, to exhort one another, to provoke one another to love and good works" (10:24) or "Let us consider one another in order to stir up" as the New King James renders it. We must carefully consider, and diligently study, how we may stimulate one another to obedience. The goal then of the exhorter is not to simply cheer up, calm down, or bring conviction of sin to another person. The goal is not merely to change his emotional state or convince his mind of the necessity of obedience; he must be actually moved to obey. Biblical encouragement is more than giving a hopeful word when another is downcast. It is rather to speak and live so that our friends are not only cheered and strengthened while running their race or persuaded that running is good exercise, but that they are actually stirred to rise and run the race with us to the end. This is an admirable goal, but to explain it and to attain it are two quite different matters. I will offer here four ways in which we can spur those around us to love and good works.

Do Not Forsake the Assembling...

We should first encourage one another by conscientiously attending the official gatherings of our congregation. Many people know the "provoke and stir up" principle of Hebrews 10:24, but they often seem to ignore the very next verse, where the author actually advises us *how* to follow his instruction. It is not something we might immediately think of, but on reflection it shows a profound wisdom: "do not forsake the assembling of yourselves together, as the manner of some is." Going to church—participating in the corporate worship of the saints of God—is our first God-given means of mutual encouragement and exhortation. Everyone acknowledges that attendance of worship is not optional because Christ has commanded and called us to gather in His presence, and no true believer will dare or desire to stay away from His call. We need no other motivation than that, but interestingly in this passage, it is not given as a reason to come to church. We come because it is one of the best ways to encourage one another. We do not meet with Christ for our own benefit but because of His command and because it is a way to profit others. Any good we receive is a side-effect of the blessing we give to others by worshiping with them. As always in the Christian life, it is better to give than to receive, and by giving we receive.

We should not come to church with the sole intention of being filled with grace and love from others; we should come because we are already overflowing and cannot wait to give. But when we do need to be lifted up, there are few things more encouraging than to hear our brethren rejoicing in the worship of God, receiving the Word with reverence and awe, and singing from the heart with strength and feeling. I think most of us have had the unpleasant experience of attending a congregation where the hymns are mumbled and drowned in the organ, and every verse seems to be a just so much slow and painful torture. Such an atmosphere kills all encouragement, and although it may provoke us, it is probably not unto love and good works. Vigorous and joyful praise is an altogether different experience, which can encourage us and give us life even when we enter worship feeling decidedly dead, which probably happens more often than we would like to acknowledge. Some Sundays, you must admit, you don't feel like going to church: you may be tired, or not feeling well, or the children may be behaving more like wild animals than usual. You do manage to arrive on time, but with great effort, and you hope that everyone appreciates the trouble and travail you have gone through to do so. This is certainly not the best attitude to have at worship, but you are ready to buckle down and go through with it. Then suddenly something extraordinary happens. You sit down next to your friends and they start singing out like they actually mean it. They give a resounding *Amen* to the opening call to worship; they are excited, engaged, and ready to be involved. In this way they begin to work on your spirit, and you begin to realize that they have it right and you have it all wrong. Their way is the way things are supposed to be. So the Lord uses our friends to stir us up and put us in the proper frame of mind, conforming us to the proper perspective on life and worship. More often that we know, He works in this way to build us up and bring us closer to Himself.

We cannot always be the passive receivers of others' encouragement. It is equally important for us to sing out, to be heard, and to take part, for just as God uses our friends to lift us up, so also He may be using each of us to stir up other people sitting nearby, across the aisle, or across the room. I recall one little old lady at a congregation where I served, who was very sweet, but had a physical problem which caused her to fall asleep whenever she sat down for any length of time. She was very embarrassed about it, and she did everything possible to stay awake. She did not enjoy coffee but she would drink it on Sunday mornings and do everything she could think of to prevent herself from sleeping. But every time she would fall asleep anyway, and she would always apologize to me afterward and tell me that she believed that the sermon had been good one, judging from the responses she heard from other people. One day she told me, "I am going to be here every Sunday, because it is important for the young people to see that if I can come, they can come. I want to be here as an example to them. And I hope I don't fall asleep." Most of us might be tempted to laugh at the "example" she set, but in her resolve she showed a deeper understanding of the problem. She was getting very little out of worship for herself, nothing in fact but the knowledge that she was obeying the Lord and encouraging her brothers and sisters. She received nothing for herself but she gave all that was in her power to give, and God blessed her, and used her in mighty ways to bless the whole congregation.

The one who avoids church because he does not "get much out of it" has a fundamentally selfish and unChristian attitude. We do not worship to fulfill our own needs; we are there for the sake of others and for our duty to God. He deserves our presence and our hearts, whether or not He is pleased to give us anything, for He is certainly not obliged to do so. Our friends and brothers in Christ need our support in worship whether or not they are able to support us in turn. We give without expecting to receive, but the wonderful truth is that we always receive more than we give, whether we realize it or not. God is always pleased to give us more than we give Him because He is good. We all give to one another as we are able, and each person we meet gives us something different. But we can neither give nor receive if we refuse to meet together with the brethren. The command of Hebrews stands: Do not forsake the assembling of yourselves together.

Greet One Another With a Holy Kiss

The second way we encourage one another is through visible manifestations of our mutual love. This is one of my favorite themes, and I realize how often I seem to return to it, but if Scripture (and especially Paul) constantly repeat teaching on the subject, there can be no harm in my doing so. It is not enough to work up a pleasant feeling in one's heart and call it a love for the brethren; love must be manifested in an open, visible, sacrificial, and effective way. This explains the frequency of Paul's exhortation to "Greet one another with a holy kiss." He is referring to the tradition in the ancient Near East which obliged men to greet other men and women to greet other women, with a kiss on the cheek. Paul believed that this was an important thing to do—that a seemingly trivial custom was a significant part of Christian living. An especially interesting passage where this is mentioned is 2 Corinthians 13:11: "Finally, brethren, farewell. Become complete. Be of good comfort, be of one mind, live in peace; and the God of love and peace will be with you." Paul here runs through fundamental principles of Christian fellowship and sanctification: maturity, unity of mind and spirit, and the bond of peace; but as if these were not enough, he concludes in the next verse: "Greet one another with a holy kiss." The unity and peace of the saints cannot exist on paper only. It has to be openly expressed in a visible, physical way.

When applying this passage to our own situation, the particular form of greeting is not as important as the principle involved. It does not matter so much *how* we express the union and peace of the saints, but it does matter *that* we do express it in some way appropriate to our time and place. The obligation to express love should be esteemed as seriously as the obligation to possess love. We are not ethereal spirits but mysterious fusions of body and soul, and we require concrete, down-to-earth expressions and actions because they can speak louder and more clearly than a thousand words. In the Near East, then and now, the holy kiss of women greeting other women and men other men, was such an expression. In contemporary America, however (perhaps excluding Hollywood), this is not a generally accepted custom, but the embrace between women and the handshake between men perform much the same function. In the early church, the holy kiss was the obvious expression of love, and it did not pass unnoticed among the unbelievers of their day. It was amazing to the Greco-Roman world that there could be a completely heterogeneous group of people, unconnected ethnically, socially, or geographically, who could still care so deeply about each other. It was something new and unusual in their world, and given the violence and individualism in our own culture, the love of Christians today should be a testimony equally powerful. The Puritans had a proverb: "the oil of friendship is the grace of holy affection." The oil of friendship, the substance that makes friendships run smoothly, is the grace of holy affection—love both felt and acted upon.

The Pursuit of Hospitality

The third aspect of biblical encouragement and exhortation is an aggressive concern for hospitality. Paul, in Romans 12:10 and following, is winding up his epistle, giving out a flurry of one-line exhortations: "Be kindly affectionate to one another with brotherly love, in honor giving preference to one another; not lagging in diligence, fervent in spirit, serving the Lord; rejoicing in hope, patient in tribulation, continuing steadfastly in prayer; distributing to the needs of the saints." He finally comes in verse thirteen to— "given to hospitality." The word *given* here is the same word that is translated elsewhere as *persecute*. In fact, it is the same word used by Paul in Acts 26:11, describing his former life as an unbeliever: "And I punished them often in every synagogue and compelled them to blaspheme; and being exceedingly enraged against them, I *persecuted* them even to foreign cities." We come to the surprising conclusion that our zeal for hospitality should be as intense as Paul's Pharisaical zeal was against the Christians; we are to *persecute* hospitality (in a way which, we hope, will be pleasing rather than alarming to our guests). According to Paul, we must be aggressive rather than passive in our pursuit of hospitality. When you want to get to know someone, you don't stand around waiting for them to come to you. You pursue them, invite them, take the initiative, and, in short, show yourself to be friendly. We are to initiate hospitality rather than standing about, waiting to be included in someone else's.

Reluctance at this point may spring from the belief that one has inadequate resources or circumstances to be hospitable. You may live in a small apartment rather than a house, or you are not an experienced cook, or you did not grow up among hospitable people, and so everything seems a little awkward. These can be legitimate concerns, but all of them really miss the true meaning of hospitality. Hospitality need not involve spending a great amount of money on a fancy meal, although fancy meals certainly enhance it. It does not require a nice home or a nice setting, although these are fine and pleasant things to have. The focus of hospitality is neither on the full table or the large room but on the open door. An open door is more than sufficient evidence that you have a godly concern for your friends, and that is better than any feast. "Better is a dinner of herbs"—in the South, we would say "greens"—"Better is a dinner of herbs where love is, than a fatted calf with hatred" (Prov. 15:17). Because love so far surpasses hate, a little plate of vegetables can far surpass the ancient equivalent of a huge barbecue. The hungry soul is satisfied with very little physical food when it is seasoned by biblical love, as another proverb says: "Better is a dry morsel with quietness than a house full of feasting with strife" (Prov. 17:1). A house full of feasting cannot compare with a dry wafer accompanied by biblical contentment and true love.

The heart of hospitality is the encouragement of others. The Scriptures assume that God's people often come together for this reason. This is why Paul, in nearly all of his epistles, exhorts believers to be patient, longsuffering, thoughtful, kind, and gentle with one another. He does this because he knows they are gathering together but having a rough time with it, aggravating instead of encouraging one another. But they were gathering together—if they were not, they would not have to be patient. Most of us are patient with ourselves, and we can usually learn to get along with our family or those whom we live with. But when large groups of sinners come together, they need forbearance, patience, a bit of a thick skin, and all the other qualities that Paul commands. It is the Lord's will that we be often together, and He ministers to us in this way, allowing us, figuratively speaking, to bump our heads, dent fenders, and put a few scratches in each other's paint. It sharpens us and makes us grow in grace. It is necessary for our sanctification. One who refrains from communing with others will suffer much more than these little annoyances.

In encouraging the saints to hospitality, I do not suggest that every minute of our schedules needs to be filled with parties, dinners, and receptions. Hospitality should be a regular part of our routine, though we are not obliged to exert it on a fixed schedule, daily or even weekly. However, although biblical friendship does not require a great deal of money, it does require an investment of time and godly concern for others. It is no good to excuse yourself by saying that you do not have the time for it. If you truly do not have the time for it, then you are simply too busy, and ought to adjust your schedule accordingly. Friendliness is too important to sacrifice for your own selfish concerns. Hospitality is a worthier goal to pursue aggressively than any ambition. Whether or not you are a good cook or have a nice home, you are obligated to have a willingness to spend time with the brethren. Do not complain about having no friends if you are unwilling to perform one of the most basic duties of friendship: the vigorous persecution of hospitality.

The Mouth of the Righteous

The fourth means of encouragement is edifying conversation. Everyone should memorize Proverbs 18:21: "Death and life are in the power of the tongue, and those who love it will eat its fruit." Our words are powerful, able either to deaden or enliven others. Therefore we must be sure that our conversation is profitable and life-giving. "The mouth of the righteous is a well of life, but violence covers the mouth of the wicked" (Prov. 10:11). The mouth can be like a shaft to the refreshing waters of a wise soul, or it can be a means of violence, deceiving and blocking off access to the water. And Proverbs 10:21: "The lips of the righteous feed many, but fools die for lack of wisdom"—the words of the righteous are a life-giving food. "There is one who speaks like the piercing of a sword, but the tongue of the wise promotes salvation." The last word is often translated "health" but I believe "salvation" is better. A wise tongue promotes wholeness and helps others in a saving way. "Anxiety in the heart of man causes depression, a good word makes it glad" (Prov. 12:25). Christians need not consult secular psychology when the Scriptures give us all the wisdom we need. An anxious and depressed man does not need six to ten weeks of therapy; he needs a "good word." This does not mean we should tell him a good joke. A good word is a holy word, a word that suits his situation, a word of encouragement or exhortation, rebuke or comfort, whatever his need may be. The good word is the word that deals with the problem—the anxiety that is causing his depression. The good word addresses the problem and makes him glad.

We can see from these proverbs how words give both life and death. For this reason Paul exhorts the Ephesians in this way: "Let no corrupt communication proceed out of your mouth, but that which is good for the use of edifying, that it may minister grace to the hearers" (4:29). Our words either minister grace to others or they spread iniquity. Young people, and especially young men, need to hear Paul's rebuke on this subject. It is easy to become careless with your words and the language that you use. Language is important. What you say when you are frustrated—e.g., when you hit your finger with a hammer—is important because it shows something about your heart. With our words we continually either minister grace or spread iniquity. Coarse language spreads iniquity, defiling others, and those who use it become not a well of life, but a hose full of mud, spattering all those within hearing. Our words either build up the faith of others or undermine it. Therefore, if we are to cultivate godly friendships, one of the chief ingredients will be edifying conversation. But what exactly is edifying conversation? What kind of conversation ministers grace to its hearers? What should we talk about when we are together? Obviously we should talk about everything. We are not those Christians who think it is wrong to talk about this or that subject. The whole earth is the Lord's and we can talk about it all. We can talk about sports, weather, news, or anything else, as long as we talk about it in a certain way and from a certain perspective.

Of course there are some things that we should always try to include in our conversations, and although we cannot include all them at once, we should habitually incorporate them into our daily speech. According to the Scriptures, we should regularly rehearse the mercies of God, so that we do not forget His benefits and kindness to us. "Bless the Lord, O my soul, and forget not all His benefits" (Ps. 103:1). We should often review with others God's wise dealings with us. "I will meditate also on all thy work, and talk of thy doings" (Ps. 77:12). David promises not only to meditate on the works of God, but also to talk about them, and we assume he will not be talking to himself. He wants to discuss his meditations with all of his friends, benefiting them and receiving also the benefit of their responses. We all see God's work in nature and revelation in different ways, and we should use what we see to help others. God instructs us through the shared thoughts and mediations of others. How many times have you seen the Scriptures or the works of God in an entirely new way, because of the shared meditations of others? It is good and right for us to rehearse God's mercies in our communion together.

We should also discuss the truth of God—the doctrines and theology which deepen and clarify our understanding and appreciation of his gracious works toward us. So many times we realize how shallow our understanding of God is, but when we talk and think about these things again and again, we find that it does grow deeper and wider over time. We want God to be big in our eyes. He is infinite, but our finitude and weakness prevents us from seeing His immensity. But as we talk about His truth, He grows bigger to us, and godly people have always had these doctrinal discussions for this very purpose—to discuss the things they have found in the Word, and by sharing them, deepen and widen each other's understanding of God. "I will bless the Lord at all times; His praise shall continually be in my mouth. My soul will make its boast in the Lord, and the humble shall hear of it and be glad. O magnify the

Lord with me, let us exalt His name together" (Ps. 34:1–3). David is not talking about his private quiet time or private worship of God. He wants to think of God so that he can tell others, and praise Him so that others can hear. The "humble" are enlivened by it, and David spreads the joy of the gospel to them. Even if they have heard the truth before, and have known it for a long time, it makes them glad to hear someone else excited and rejoicing over it. Our conversation should delight in discussing the truths of God.

Of course, the truth is dead unless we apply it to one another, drawing out every implication for ourselves and our brethren and bringing it to bear on every aspect of our talk. Whether we are talking about the game or the news or the weather, it is profitable to view every subject from a biblical perspective, so that we train ourselves to think rightly about God's creation. Learning how to think in this way is the great benefit of godly fellowship. The world does not know how to do it, but together we are learning how—by throwing out all the old categories instilled in us by Satan, the world, and our poor education, and by being trained now to think instead from God's perspective. An example of the application of sound doctrine is in 1 Thessalonians 4, when Paul clarifies the coming of the Lord. Certain men had been making a disturbance in the church by teaching that the Lord had already come, and those who thought they had been "left behind" were understandably upset by this. Paul corrects their doctrine concerning the Lord's coming and the resurrection of the dead, and then says (4:18), "Now therefore, comfort one another with these words." He does not expect his sermonizing to be a complete solution; he urges the Thessalonians to apply these truths to one another, to talk about them and comfort each other with them. Comfort and encouragement flow from the application of true biblical teaching. Paul describes this again in 2 Corinthians 1:3–4: "Blessed be the God and Father of our Lord Jesus Christ, the Father of mercies and God of all comfort, who comforts us in all our tribulation, that we may be able to comfort those who are in any trouble, with the comfort with which we ourselves are comforted by God." Whenever we must endure tribulation, we are forced to think through the things of God, and as a result God comforts us. He comforts us so that we may in turn comfort others in the same way. By speaking of God's work in our own lives, we are able to do His work in the lives of others; this is especially true of ministers and elders in the congregation. We should discuss and apply the truth to one another.

Exhorting one another to love and good deeds is a key ingredient of true friendship and mutual communion. No friendship is profitable to me if I am not being provoked to love and good deeds through it. If it is not profitable, then I need either to restructure the parameters of that friendship or break it off all together. If I am not being provoked to love and good works, then I am being provoked toward backsliding, stagnation, and rebellion. No friendship holds its participants in neutral. If a relationship is not provoking you to holiness, it is provoking you to unholiness, and if it cannot be changed it must be dissolved; we may not maintain any unbiblical friendship. Now is the time to apply these things to yourself and to your relationships. Is this the kind of friendship you have with other people, one that provokes yourself and others to love and good works? Is there just dealing? Is there holy compassion? Is there thoughtful sensitivity? Is there unflinching loyalty? Is there earnest encouragement? If not, then that relationship is an unprofitable acquaintance but it is not a true, biblical friendship. Rather than being helped by this association, you are probably being greatly damaged. To not increase in love and good works is increase in sin and ungodliness.

One of the greatest blessings of the gospel is that we receive the peace and comfort of Christ not only for ourselves as individuals, but also as members of a community who can enjoy them with us. When someone experiences a great event alone, he can never fully communicate that experience to others, and that fact can actually spoil his own experience of it. The greatest experiences are those we can share with other people, and the glory of the gospel is that it extends to a whole household of faith, which will one day encompass the entire world. It must have been a thrilling, delightful, and comforting surprise to the Ephesians (who were Gentiles as we are), when Paul, a Jew and an apostle of God, said to them: "Now, therefore, you are no more strangers and foreigners, but fellow citizens with the saints and of the household of God" (Eph. 2:19). A few years earlier the Jews would have called these people dogs, but now the great Apostle calls them brothers, and assures them that by faith they have been brought into the chosen household of God! They were once strangers, far off, isolated, alone in the darkness of unbelief, and now they are fellow citizens with the saints in the New Jerusalem. They can now share in the great comfort and blessedness of being in a vast company of believers who love the same righteousness, who love and delight in the same Savior, who are bound in the same direction, and who are glad to help them along in the way. Those of us who were once far off, and who know what it is like to be all alone, find particular comfort here. God puts the solitary into families—that is the gospel. Let us then take advantage of this as best we can, building our friendships in the household of faith, so that we can walk in the way of life with joy and gladness, rejoicing daily, encouraging and provoking one another always to love and good works.

Chapter 5
Destroying Friendships

Nothing is more conducive to our comfort, encouragement, and protection than godly companions. God has ordained that His mercies be dispensed through human instruments, and this is most commonly done through those brethren and friends that God gives us. In a very real sense, we shall never be what we ought to be apart from faithful friends. I have dwelt so far on the positive qualities of friends and friendships, but this is clearly insufficient to a full understanding of the matter at hand. In this chapter I want to fill in this gap and conclude our study of biblical friendship by considering those things that can destroy it. God warns us against three things which are destructive of biblical relationships.

A Loose Tongue

Friendships can weather all manner of adversity, but they cannot stand against this adversary. Remember that "life and death are in the power of the tongue" (Prov. 18:21). The degree of damage or good that a person can do, just by how he speaks to others, is astounding and should never be underestimated. We must avoid all manner of evil speaking, that is, any destructive use of the tongue. Such speaking takes on a number of different forms, but there are a few major ones that we should particularly identify and avoid.

First, we ought to avoid slander and gossip. Again, the book of Proverbs are rich mine of wisdom in these matters: "A perverse man sews strife, and a whisperer separates the best of friends" (Prov. 16:28). Even the closest, most intimate friends can be separated by evil whisperings. In the previous verse, we find "An ungodly man digs up evil, and it is on his lips like a burning fire." The person with an undisciplined tongue is like a flame thrower, starting fires everywhere, burning things down, especially burning up bridges of relationships. James recalls the language of this proverb: "And the tongue is a fire, a world of iniquity. The tongue is so set among our members that it defiles the whole body, and sets on fire the course of nature; and it is set on fire by hell" (3:6). Tongues, like flames, can cause incredible damage; the unbridled tongue will destroy everywhere it goes. The one who spreads rumors and gossip is described as a vicious one, a perverse one, the one who seeks to undermine good things and who has no sense of biblical propriety. This person loves to dig up evil and spread it as far as he can. Romans classifies the rumor-monger as having a depraved mind, included in the list of those kinds of people who are given over to their own lust. "And even as they did not like to retain God in their knowledge, God gave them over to a debased mind, to do those things which are not fitting; being filled with all unrighteousness, sexual immorality, wickedness, covetousness, maliciousness; full of envy, murder, strife, deceit, evil-mindedness; they are *whisperers*, *backbiters*, haters of God, violent, proud, boasters, inventors of evil things..." (Rom. 1:28–30). God has given the evil speaker over to a debased mind, utterly abandoning him to self-destruction. He takes the sins of the tongue very seriously. It is a rule which must be made into a habit of mind.

In Proverbs 24:28–29, the writer gives us this exhortation: "Do not be a witness against your neighbor without a cause, for would you deceive with your lips? Do not say, 'I will do to him just as he has done to me. I will render to the man according to his works.'" We dare not slander another man or reveal things against others unnecessarily. Certainly, sometimes we do have to speak of the sins of others, when it is required for justice or discipline, or by our obligation to rebuke them in love. But ordinarily we are not to speak of these evil things, even if they are true—for there is a way to slander someone even by speaking the truth about them. We should recognize this kind of wickedness for what it really is—hatred of our neighbor—and have zero tolerance for all kinds of slander and gossip.

Another kind of evil speech not so easily detected, and if it is, does not seem as repulsive as it ought to seem—I refer here to flattery. We are sometimes confused about what flattery is, but certainly it is not encouraging someone else, or giving him a sober and true evaluation of his real gifts and abilities. Flattery is not encouragement but *exaggerated* praise. Its purpose is not to encourage or build up but to manipulate. The flatterer wants his victims to feel in his debt, to owe him something for his sympathy. The flatterer builds up this debt so that he can later exploit it. He speaks highly of others so that they will feel that they should speak highly of him. Flattery is selfishness, and God strongly warns against it many times in Scripture. Consider the well-known (but narrowly interpreted) Proverbs 27:14: "He who blesses his friend with a loud voice, rising early in the morning, it will be counted a curse to him." Of course it has a great *prima facie* application for us non-morning-people; the guy who gets up at the crack of dawn and starts talking loudly, telling jokes, and thinking he is hilarious at six a.m. is in the same class as someone who screams out offensive curses. Certainly it is comforting that wise men, in all ages, don't find very many things funny at six a.m. But this interpretation of the proverb, though humorous as an evening-person "proof text," is not adequate and distracts from the main sense of the text. The phrase "loud voice" refers to exaggerated language, and thus he who blesses his friend in an exaggerated way is a curse to his friend. The wise man recognizes bloated praise and knows exactly what it really is.

In seminary, we had the opportunity in chapel one day of hearing a famous guest preacher. We were all eagerly looking forward to his sermon, but the man who introduced him did so in such a way that terribly embarrassed the speaker and just about everyone else who was present. He said that he had always longed to hear this man preach, that he was the greatest preacher alive, and that he moved audiences in ways they have never been moved before. He continued in this manner for some time, until the whole audience was quite uneasy for the speaker's sake. Fortunately for him and for us, he happened to be a Scot—and I think it is a good rule of thumb never to flatter a Scottish preacher. He rose to speak, cast a glance at his host, and said, without much ceremony, "With that introduction, my address is now doomed to disappoint you, for it is impossible that any mere man could live up to such praise." I wanted to tell him that he had hit the nail exactly on the head. The unfortunate host deserved whatever he got because the kind of flattery he gave was counted as a curse.

Of course, it is not wrong to bless our friends and express our thankfulness for them, but extravagant, inflated praises gauged to impress them or others should be condemned as flattery. The genuine expression of appreciation is always proper and too often neglected, and warnings against flattery should not make us shy away from honest praise. How many times are we helped by others and yet never tell them how we appreciate them? It is important for us to be grateful and to publicly acknowledge the good work of others. I have often written letters to the authors of good books I have read, if they are still living, to thank them for what they had done, and it was a great joy to express my gratitude to them. Such expressions are necessary for building up our fellow believers and for keeping us aware of our dependence on others.

Flattery, on the other hand, is neither encouragement, nor gratitude, nor appreciation, but sheer wickedness. Far from being an expression of friendliness, it only serves to undermine and destroy it. "A man who flatters his neighbor spreads a net for his feet" (Prov. 29:5). Flattery is a dangerous snare and an act of violence. The person may not mean to hurt his neighbor by it, but we must realize that the audience of flattery is always a sinner, and sinners tend to receive exaggerated praise as basically accurate. We love to think more highly of ourselves than we ought to, and even if we ostensibly do not, when someone begins to throw fragrant bouquets of sweet talk at our feet, it is easy to shrug and think, "I never suspected I was so great, but if other people say I am, I suppose they must be right." That is precisely the danger of the snare—that people will actually believe their sycophants. We must learn to recognize them as enemies and not as friends.

These issues are especially important to apply in regard to young children. Though they need love and encouragement, it is unnecessary and even destructive to exaggerate their abilities and gifts. We need not swoon over every little thing they do in order to encourage them. Such spoiling will only tend to create a petty, proud, deluded little fiend, who thinks he is the greatest blessing to the world and that everything he does is automatically wonderful. Children are sinners like everyone else, and they believe what foolish adults tell them. Therefore we should take care to be very honest in our praise of them. Whether at recitals, sports events, or academic ceremonies, when they make a genuine effort and perform as well as they know how, we ought not rave about it as if it were the most beautiful song, fastest race, or eloquent speech we have ever witnessed. Often such praise is given because the performance was poor, and we do not quite know what to say to them afterward. Of course, if they made no real effort and failed, they should be rebuked for their laziness, but a real effort deserves measured praise and appreciation, if only for the sake of the effort; if the performance itself is also successful, the child deserves somewhat more praise according to his or her capacity and accomplishment. That sort of praise is encouraging, but very rare is the prodigy who deserves to be praised like a professional. Do not lie to your children in your assessment of their talents; when they do a poor job, do not tell them that it was great. You need not be brutally honest, failing to "consider their frame," but you can say many things more accurate than "it was great." We must thread a fine line between crushing the spirits of children and inflating their opinion of themselves, which sets them up to be crushed later on. Both errors are equally destructive to the child, and this will rebound as a curse to his parents.

And so flatterers of friends and children are not acting as friends but as enemies. "A lying tongue hates those who are crushed by it, and a flattering mouth works ruin" (Prov. 26:28). In the parallelism of this verse, the lying tongue is set in parallel with the flattering mouth: the lying tongue hates the man to whom he is lying, and similarly the flatterer hates the man that he is flattering. Flattery is an expression of hatred, despite the people who, blinded by them, see them as sensitive, wise, insightful, discerning, loving, and delightful. Thus God says that He hates those who flatter. Part of loving one's neighbor is telling them the truth. A.W. Pink once said, "The man who loves me the most is the one who tells me the most truth about myself." The flatterer loves only himself and wants others to love him too. He gives the cheap gift of words, expecting to receive an expensive sacrifice of friendship, and that is the heart of his manipulation. He does not care that he might destroy others in this, or that he is spreading a trap for them, because he is too occupied with himself. Thus we have a strange paradox: the world loves the flatterer, but the flatterer hates the world; he has many friends but he seeks to destroy them all.

If we are to have biblical friendships and relationships, we must avoid both flattery and the flatterer, and all loose talk. "He who goes about as a talebearer reveals secrets; therefore do not associate with one who flatters with his lips" (Prov. 20:19). Again, notice the parallel structure of the proverb, which here associates the flatterer with the talebearer, and both of them we should avoid, for God will judge all loose tongues. The psalmist says, "Help, Lord, for the godly man ceases, the faithful disappear from among the sons of men. They speak idly everyone with his neighbor, with flattering lips and with a double heart they speak" (Ps. 12:1–3). He laments that the godly and faithful have disappeared from the world, but how does he recognize this? The ungodly reveal themselves by their idle speech, flattery, and lies. The right response to this situation is an imprecatory prayer for God to destroy the destroyers: "May the Lord cut off all flattering lips, and the tongue that speaks proud things." God will judge every idle word that comes out of our mouths; therefore be careful. Do not think that little gossips and white lies are small or inconsequential things. Weigh your words carefully, and say what ought to be said and no more. Loose, undisciplined tongues destroy friendships.

Forbearance and Charity

It should be obvious that all of our friends in this life are sinners. Angels, at least in this life, are not permitted to befriend us in the way we have been considering here. They are certainly ministering spirits to the people of God, but do not have personal knowledge of them; they are not introduced to us, we cannot converse with them, and so forth. So all true friendships must be between sinners, and forbearance is the quality that makes such relationships possible. Regardless of any good intentions, sinners will have conflict with one another. We do not desire conflict, but friendship in this life implies it. Forbearance and charitable judgments allow conflict to be resolved and so allows friendships to survive and prosper. Without this key ingredient, the relationship will not cohere against conflicting forces. Scripture expresses this by portraying patient forbearance with others' sins and infirmities as a prominent demand of love. "Hatred stirs up strife, but love covers all sins" (Prov. 10:12). And Peter echoes this wisdom: "Above all things have fervent love for one another, for love will cover a multitude of sins" (1 Pet. 4:8). Forbearance is then one important application of love. It is not part of our obligation in friendship to point out each and every shortcoming or inconsistency in the lives and characters of our friends.

It is no person's business to act as the conscience of another. To quote a rather picturesque proverb one friend of mine once told me, "You don't have to jump on every flea that falls off the dog." The point is that there are a whole lot of fleas on any one dog, and if someone believes himself called to kill each one that he sees, upon everyone near him, then soon he will be able to do nothing else, and other people will begin to avoid him. The flea-catcher has few friends.

Clearly I don't mean that we can ignore one another's sins; we all know the Bible better than that, and we know the proper place of a loving rebuke. But the Bible strikes a balance between the two. On the one hand, we have a responsibility to help one another grow and change. On the other hand, we must recognize that sanctification is a process that takes a lifetime to complete. It takes time to work out all the crooked things that sin has worked into us. So as long as we can perceive in a friend the willingness to deal with sin, we should be patient with him, helping him deal with the sin little by little, so as not to dishearten or overwhelm but rather help bear his infirmities. As Paul says, "We who are strong ought to bear with the infirmities of the weak" (Rom. 15:1). It can be tempting to do this for our own pleasure and satisfaction, and sometimes it is very pleasing to point out another's wrinkles, but Paul tells us to do more than point—we must carry some of the burden ourselves.

So we recognize that sanctification takes time, and we must leave room for the Spirit to work. We must be willing to allow one another time to grow in grace. To refuse it and to demand (in effect) instant universal sanctification is disheartening and only stirs up strife. It gives a person the wrong perspective on friendship. We don't want to play the spiritual cosmetic surgeon, looking upon every blemish with twitching fingers, feeling that our duty is to correct it. Some of the more serious and glaring blemishes do require a word or action, and Scripture demands that we not ignore these. But for the smaller and secondary things, we should allow more time, so as not to dishearten others with harsh criticisms.

We often see the other person's faults far more clearly than he sees them, but we need to give place to the Spirit, waiting patiently for sanctification work itself out and helping him along little by little (as we trust he will also do for us). If we do this, eventually he will uncover and repair his minor defects on his own. Friendships are in danger when someone tries to be the great spiritual cosmetic surgeon, apparently believing himself to be God's great gift to his friends, charged and empowered to straighten them all out. Such foolishness is not an adequate foundation for holy friendship.

How do these principles come into play in real life? How exactly should Christians exercise forbearance? In the first place, forbearance means that we must not allow ourselves to be sensitive to every perceived slight we receive from others, after they receive our advice. Whether the slight is real or imagined—and sometimes it is impossible to know the difference—do not break off fellowship with those who do not respond as you thought they should or as you had hoped. Perhaps they do not agree with you about what is a defect and what is not, and you disagree about how Scripture applies to it. Not everyone (including yourself) has the wisdom to give *and* receive rebuke perfectly, and we should be careful not to take offense, and sacrifice fellowship for our wounded pride.

Second, we must not form rash judgments against one another. Do not be quick to read evil motives into the words, expressions, or actions of other people: "Let none of you think evil in your heart against your neighbor" (Zech. 8:17). We so often want to interpret things this way. But only when there are no other options, when there is no ambiguity, should we be forced to that option. Always give the benefit of a charitable judgment unless there is indisputable evidence to the contrary. Love "thinks no evil" (1 Cor. 13:4)

We may not be defensive when others disagree with us on matters of secondary importance and on truly debatable issues. Many things about Christian life and thought are not debatable. The Bible is a clear revelation and the vast majority of topics and issues are actually quite easily settled by reference to the Scriptures. Yet we also recognize that all things are not equally plain to us, as the Westminster Confession says. These things are plainly revealed, but we do not understand them as clearly as other issues, and so at those points we must not become fanatic about our own little convictions. In issues over which godly Christians disagree and have in the past disagreed, we must not be offended when others fail to see it as we do. This sort of disagreement may be holy and sincere. Two Christians may study the Scriptures diligently, seeking to understand and apply it, and on certain unclear issues they may draw very different conclusions. They do not wish to create divisions in the body of Christ, but they seek to follow the will of God on this subject. Clearly this is a holy disagreement, which is actually good for the health of those two believers and of the church as a whole. This kind of issue keeps us in good shape theologically, so that we do not embrace things that sound good but are not, depend too much on our own instincts and first impressions of truth, or jump to unjustified conclusions. It forces us to be sure of our convictions before we hold them too firmly. This is an important safeguard for us, and should never be despised.

If a believer were to surround himself only with those who agreed with him on every particular of the faith, he would never grow in understanding. He would be "right" about everything, never knowing whether or not he held certain wrong or indefensible positions. Holy differences are means by which we grow in our understanding and discernment, clarifying and solidifying the understanding of our faith. Sometimes *un*holy disagreements can do the same—if those who are more holy respond properly to them. Forbearance in these matters is essential. When this is lacking, it is impossible for biblical friendships to prosper. If you only want friends who will always agree with you, you will never have any true friends. Even if you could find someone to be your yes-man, you would soon find him to be a very boring person. We desire to learn the truth and it is not helpful to avoid these differences. We must learn to see the good side of our differences.

Immature Reconciliations

This brings us to last thing that will destroy biblical friendship: refusal to deal biblically with sin. Sin not only separates us from God—it separates us from each other. Since God is the one who saves us from the power of sin, for biblical friendship to thrive we must deal with sin in God's way. There is no way around the problem of sin between friends; we are dealing with fellow sinners, and we will inevitably sin. The only question is, How we will deal with it? There is no way around God's solution to the problem, except perhaps the patch-up job done by walking away from a fight until everyone cools off and then guiltily and awkwardly moping back together when scabs and scars cover the wounds. That is not the way we ought to live together. No Christian wants or needs that kind of shallow and messy relationship. Instead, we ought to deal faithfully with one another, so that everytime one friend offends another, each one is obliged to seek reconciliation *no matter whose fault it was*. For the one who committed the offense, the Bible teaches in Matthew 5 that if he remembers what he has done against his brother, he must go to him to seek reconciliation. Matthew 18 teaches that when someone realizes that another has sinned against him, the offended one should go to the offender. *You* (whoever *you* are, whether the offender or the victim) should always seek out your friend, and with this double responsibility to reconcile, many offenses are settled with love.

When there is friction between two believers, the one who was in the right should not justify himself and fall into self-righteousness. That attitude of wounded pride wants the offender to come to him, begging for forgiveness, and ignores the responsibility of both parties to seek harmony. Some are tempted to simply ignore these real offenses instead of facing them, but this attitude fosters the growth of bitterness. They are tempted to talk to everyone about the offender except the offender himself, and such talk is unloving toward him. We are not to give unnecessary publicity to our brother's sin. "He who covers a transgression seeks love, but he who

repeats a matter separates friends" (Prov. 17:9). The one who talks
unnecessarily about another's sin seeks to estrange him from the
rest of his friends, just as he and the gossiper have already been
estranged from one another. More friendships are destroyed in this
way than in any other. More churches are destroyed by this one error
than by any other. Because this is a very serious and constant danger,
I and many others have a great and continual fear that it might
spring up in our own congregations, and thus I make it a point to
warn against it regularly from the pulpit. It may not be tolerated.
Satan loves to destroy congregations through this kind of discord,
but if we resist him, we can have a powerful influence, by the blessing of God, through growing in love and forbearance. If we fail to
resist as we ought, being neither careful nor zealous in our respon-
sibilities to the community, we must be aware that many labors of
love, unity, and forbearance can be lost in the course of a single
evening. Beware of refusing to deal with sin biblically, for it divides
friends, and divided friends divide also the body of Christ.

The Great Value of True Friendship

Now we come back full circle and recognize once more the great
value of true friendship. Strangely and sadly, it is becoming rarer in
this modern world as in our culture the covenant breaks down, and
the influence of Christianity begins to wane in the West. There will
be some who live and die without ever having a true friend. Friendship is impossible apart from Christianity; unbelievers can have
friends because they pretend to act like Christians in this respect.
Realistically, they can keep their friendships as long as they act like
Christians together, which means they often do not keep them long,
having only a series of brief but explosive relationships. Apart
from some presence of the gospel, sinners cannot truly befriend one
another.

Because of this necessary gospel influence, the church is the most basic and important model for all communities and friendships. In every age, but particularly in ours, it is the rare and vital place in this world where we can cultivate deep friendships and find trusted counselors, a blessing beyond our comprehension. It is impossible to overstate the value of such a community, where friendships are built with the protection of biblical oversight. When things go wrong, and we are hurt by those whom we trusted, we always have a way of appeal and restoration, because both friends are under a common authority. Such protection frees us to pursue all kinds of biblical relationships on all different levels of intimacy. We can give ourselves to others, not having to worry about being betrayed, taken advantage of, or (figuratively speaking) knifed in the back, because we are bound in a covenant of love. If one of our friends does break that covenant, we will not be abandoned; the offender will be held accountable, being restored or harmony or unmasked for what he truly is and put out where he can do no more damage. This kind of protective community is one of the greatest and most necessary gifts God has given us.

"Where there is no counsel, the people fall, but in the multitude of counselors there is safety" (Prov. 11:14). No one knows enough to live, thrive, and grow by himself; we all must have wise and godly people whom we trust to lead and guide us. "Without counsel plans go awry, but in the multitude of counselors they are established" (Prov. 15:22). In the church, we have an opportunity to create a place of safety, a place where holy purposes are established and come to pass, a place where healing and salvation abound, a place where there are no strangers, and where nobody is truly alone. This is our labor and glory, but unless we diligently fulfill the duties of friendship, all will be lost. Unless we avoid loose tongues, and unless we exercise forbearance and a willingness to deal with sin in God's way, we will have nothing.

We must at some time reckon with the realities of the covenant: we are fellow citizens of the household of God. We belong now to one family, and that is most emphatically not a cute, catchy way to refer to the church, but soberly represents the reality of our relations. We are a family, and we have to deal with one another in that way. We are not *a* family, but *the* family. God is the Father and He is the one from whom all the families draw their names. He is supreme, and our family is supreme over all the families of the earth, being their pattern and fulfillment. We have then a blessed and priceless privilege to be a part of the church of the Lord Jesus— a privilege that we dare not despise or treat carelessly. Instead we recognize it in faith and do everything in our power to cultivate, preserve, and promote true friendliness.

We have biblical relationships for the honor of God and for the glory of His Son, and as he blesses the church, it becomes as it were a magnet in the world, attracting all the fractured and sin-scarred sinners who are by nature the same as we. In the presence of our Savior, we have also the presence of these healed people, whom we can trust and love without fear, maintaining harmony by perform-ing our duties to them in affection and receiving the same benefits back from them. Therefore, we give ourselves to building, promot-ing, and preserving godly friendships. It is the great work of love, the work which will transform ourselves, the church, and the world.

Part Two:

Hospitality

Chapter 6
Commands to Hospitality

One of my friends and fellow-pastors has often noted that individuals can live with inconsistency, but cultures cannot; every culture will eventually become consistent with its foundational principles. Many people live in a way that contradicts their professed beliefs, but societies cannot tolerate that kind of imbalance for very long. Today, we are seeing our culture becoming more and more consistent with its principles. People like to create their own little eclectic religion of independence and self-sufficiency, such as is promoted through the public schools, pop philosophy, advertising, and the general media. We all are acquainted with its mantras: "You need to be you," "You need to find yourself," "You need to be good to yourself." *You* is the key word, through which these modern proverbs enforce the blatant idolatry of self-worship and by them have damaged our society more than we can know. Self-love fractures the family, the basic unit of society. Fathers care little for their children, and husbands care little about their wives, except perhaps as household machines. This uncaring lifestyle is consistent with the idea that the self and its wants are of the highest importance.

A biblical church and her faithful people stand in stark contradiction to this idea. Unfortunately, the church at large has failed in her witness and has even led the rest of society down the path of self-love. Ministers of Christ were the first ones to preach this new gospel, and now only ministers of Christ can repudiate it and preach the true gospel. In everything a faithful church does, it must set its face against all forms of self-worship, warning of its destructiveness and eventual condemnation. The faithful church may proclaim this through the direct preaching of the gospel or by simply living the gracious and holy life which God has called us to live— a life of peace, true and principled love, real loyalty, and communion together. When God's people care for one another, it is a powerful testimony against the manifest selfishness and idolatry of the world, and it is necessary in order to give credibility to the preached word. So let's examine some of the main New Testament commands concerning hospitality. My open thanks to Alexander Strauch's work in *Hospitality Commands* for raising the various issues and scriptures that I discuss; I hope to have continued and developed some of the points begun there.

A Living Sacrifice

In Romans, Paul exhorts the whole church at Rome to be "given to hospitality." This is a good principle in itself, but we should be aware of the larger context to understand it fully. Paul has just written eleven chapters explaining the wonderful and mysterious grace of God and what that grace has accomplished for God's people. Through Christ we have been redeemed, saved, and justified, and we are now being sanctified. Then in chapter twelve, Paul begins to give particular commands on the basis of the theology and soteriology that he has just given. If God has done *this* for us, how should we now live? Notice his *therefore*—he has laid out the premises; what follows? "I beseech you therefore, brethren, by [Greek *dia*—by means of, on the basis of, through] the mercies of God, that you present your bodies a living sacrifice, holy, acceptable to God, which is your reasonable service" (Rom. 12:1). Giving oneself up to God body and soul, as a complete living sacrifice, is the only proper response to the grace of God. We can no longer can live for ourselves, but devoted to His glory. On the basis of the mercies He has shown to us, we no longer belong to ourselves, but are devoted and set apart to Him, obliged to do all and only what will bring Him glory. That is what it means to be a living sacrifice. We do this by conforming to the Word as the revealed, perfect will of God, so that we no longer conform to the world but are transformed by the Word. "Do not be conformed to this world, but be transformed by the renewing of your mind" (v. 2). It is the best way to live, and as deed joined to word, it is the only true testimony of God's grace.

This general command forms the link between the earlier chapters of theology and the following passage of practical instruction. What exactly does it mean, in real life and in definite actions, to give oneself as a living sacrifice to Christ? First of all, we should humble ourselves and think of others first. Do not think of yourself more highly (or more lowly) than you ought, but think soberly and realistically (v. 3). What else? We should recognize that God has put us in bodies and given us different personalities and gifts, and given us each a place in the body of Christ. Therefore we may neither envy or disparage another's gifts, but rejoice in every gift, whether it is our own or another's. "For as we have many members and one body, but all the members do not have the same function, so we, being many, are one body in Christ" (v. 4–5). The church is a body, and each person uses his gifts to strengthen the body, and is in turn strengthened by it, so that everyone grows up together to their fullness—fullness as individuals and fullness as a community. Next, we are to love one another sincerely: "Let love be without hypocrisy" (v. 9). In the remainder of the passage Paul expounds the meaning of sincere love. The renewed mind abhors what is evil, and clings to what is good. It honors others: "Be kindly affectionate to one another with brotherly love, in honor giving preference to one another" (v. 10). It lives faithfully in every circumstance: "Rejoicing in hope, being patient in tribulation, continuing steadfastly in prayer" (v. 12). And finally, it cares greatly for the saints: "Distributing to the needs of the saints, given to hospitality" (v. 13).

Hospitality is the primary example of meeting the needs of fellow Christians. Paul, interestingly, does not place hospitality on the periphery of essential godliness, where the modern church tends to place it. We tend to imagine it as a luxurious virtue, practiced by those who are willing and able and not required for anyone else; it is a luxury that we can occasionally afford. We certainly do not think of it as a central expression of Christian holiness and the glory of God. Paul corrects this notion. If we are not practicing hospitality, we are not loving, and when we do not love, we cease to be a living church. It is bound up with our profession of faith and our sacrifice of self to God.

Devoted to the Chase

As noted earlier, the word *given* in "given to hospitality" means to pursue tirelessly from place to place. Classical Greek writers used this word in the context of hunting; for example, it might be used to describe the attitude of a hound chasing a fox through the forest. Perhaps a better picture for us, which most of us have seen on film, is that of a cheetah chasing a gazelle. The hound is *given* to the fox, and the cheetah to the gazelle, in the sense that each is utterly devoted to the chase, concentrating all of his strength and speed on a single object. Thus when Paul says, "given to hospitality," he does not mean, "Perhaps you should be open to the possibility of being hospitable; don't refuse if you are asked." As Paul would say, may it never be! The virtue of hospitality is far from being passive. We had better go after it, chase it down, and not stop until we have wrestled it to the ground. Trying to just "let it happen" is to misunderstand and refuse to obey the command. It requires zealous, vigorous, and strenuous effort. As I have noted before, the word for *given* is translated elsewhere as "persecute," when Paul describes his former persecution of the church in Acts 26:11. He was zealous and "exceedingly enraged," and he pursued the Christians even into foreign lands, completely devoted to destroying them. After conversion, he uses the same word for the constructive devotion to hospitality. Paul did not mind the trouble of persecuting Christians; it required inconvenience, planning, time, and money. But it had become his life, because he believed it was necessary for the glory of God, and he was willing to spend any expense in pursuit of it. So often, those who do evil are more zealous for their own cause than those who do good. Paul does not want this to happen to the church. Only the active and ardent pursuit of hospitality is glorifying to God.

John Murray, in his commentary on Romans, comments on this passage in this way: "We are to be active in our pursuit of hospitality, and not merely bestowing it, perhaps grudgingly, when necessity makes it unavoidable." We begrudge hospitality more often than we would like to acknowledge. One might see a new family in church, and should feel some obligation to ask them into his home, but he waits until the last possible moment, hoping someone else will invite them first. If no one does, and if he is still feeling up to it, he then reluctantly extends the invitation. According to Paul, this "only when necessary" idea seriously misunderstands the command, the glorifying of Christ, and the grace of God in general. Does God extend his hospitality "only when necessary"? Hasn't he promised it to the whole world? "If you need me, call me" is not the spirit of Christianity. We should be hosts who earnestly seek for opportunities to show love to the brethren, and who are disappointed when not able to do so. If we have love, we do not dread it or force ourselves into it. There are two different spirits here; one of them Christian, and the other pagan. One of them glorifies Christ, the other does not. Hospitality is not an option but a holy obligation. Each Christian should pursue it, even if he were the only one in an entire congregation to do so.

The Joyful Exercise

Turning to 1 Peter 4:7–9, we find: "But the end of all things is at hand; therefore be serious and watchful in your prayers. And above all things have fervent love for one another, for 'love will cover a multitude of sins.' Be hospitable to one another without grumbling." Hospitality, according to Peter, is an obvious and preeminent fruit of biblical love for the brethren. If there is a sincere love for the brethren, there will be the joyful exercise of hospitality. It is important also to remember the context of this command. Peter was not writing to Christians who lived in times of abundance and peace; they were under a brutal and merciless persecution. "Beloved, do not think it strange concerning the fiery trial which is to try you" (v. 12). He continues to teach about suffering and judgment. He is writing to people under extreme pressure, opposition, and persecution, and some of them were even being threatened with death. In times like this, we might be tempted to think that the duty of hospitality could be suspended. If believers were being persecuted and threatened with death, distracted by suffering and trying only to stay alive from day to day, can we expect them to minister to others? According to Peter, we can and should. If there is *ever* a time when believers need to exercise hospitality, it is when they are collectively in danger; that is when everyone needs it the most. The worst thing a Christian can do during a persecution is to isolate himself from the rest of the body. The imminence of death should make love abound even more. However incredible the idea of hospitality during persecution may seem to us, it was Peter's command. These unique circumstances only highlight to a greater degree how central this virtue is to the church, for it is to be practiced at *all* times, not merely favorable ones.

Pay close attention to Peter's language in verse eight: "have *fervent* love for one another." We tend to think of a fervent emotion as one characterized only by its intensity, burning hotly but quickly. Peter is not using the word in this way; he is actually trying to convey the idea not merely of the love's intensity, but of its perseverance through hardship. This love endures, and is constant and persistent in the face of daunting obstacles, bursting through all barriers. It is essential for our love to be like this because we are sinners. When sinners are thrown together into close quarters, messes are made, conflicts arise, and love is tested. Hospitality is not some unbroken, ethereal love and joy. Real people are invited into real houses, and they have real needs that actually require some sacrifice and generosity to meet. Real people are sinners and make mistakes, perhaps saying something rude or inconsiderate, often without knowing they are hurting others. Love, if it is to survive the test of hospitality, has to be very hardy, willing to give and to cover many sins. Peter does not say that love ignores serious sin, but it does cover careless or inconsiderate words and actions. In either case, sin cannot stop love. Love rebukes great sins and covers small sins, but love always conquers sin.

In one well-known legend, Sir Walter Raleigh threw his cloak over a patch of mud so that the queen could walk over it without wetting her shoes. Christian love is, in a sense, like Raleigh's cloak. Many guests, however well-intentioned, manage to create mud-patches (whether metaphorical or literal) in their host's home. The host's duty is always to smile and throw the cloak of love over it, so that no one else is soiled by it before it can be cleaned up. All hosts must continue to cover such a guest's mud-patches, without grumbling, until he finally learns that one ought not make mud-patches in other people's houses. He needs to learn this lesson, but he cannot learn it unless others continue to treat him with kindness and grace. There will be a bit of mud thrown about, but that is the price of the lesson, both for host and guest—and the host probably learns more than the guest. This sort of hearty, gracious, patient, and fervent love is what Peter commands. It is absolutely necessary for us to have, to guard, and to keep if we are to persevere in hospitality. Love makes hospitality possible, and continued hospitality cultivates more love. This is the way a community grows. Every healthy congregation exercises pervasive and persistent hospitality.

We should always keep in mind that this obligation is for everyone. We should not quietly remain in the background if there are many other families in the church who are more hospitable than others, and who cheerfully take up our slack. No one is exempt, whether he is the only one in the congregation exercising hospitality or the only one *not* doing so. When the members of a congregation do not delight in each other's company, there is a fearful disease in that body. They have not persevered in love; their love has grown cold. Whenever there is fervent love for Christ, there will be a fervent love for His body, and the duty of hospitality will be fulfilled gladly. Peter, well aware of the difficult circumstances of his audience, exhorts them to glad obedience in this one area, which is seemingly so inconsistent with an atmosphere of persecution and danger. In all times, it is a great privilege and a great blessing. Of course it is troublesome, inconvenient, expensive, and requires hard work. Of course other people will not fully appreciate the pains one takes for them. But when we understand what a privilege it is, we will obey gladly, without the slightest hint of grumbling. Paul says that "God loves a cheerful giver." Hospitality is not a grievous burden to be dreaded, but a joyful privilege to be anticipated.

Entertaining Strangers

The last passage I will consider in this chapter is Hebrews 13:1–2: "Let brotherly love continue. Do not forget to entertain strangers, for by so doing some have unwittingly entertained angels." The apostle first exhorts the believers to "brotherly love." He commands them to love one another like their own natural siblings. This love is to continue, to persevere, to not die out. How do we keep brotherly love living and active? "Do not forget to entertain strangers." Once again, hospitality is a central expression of love in the apostle's mind. The word here that is translated as "entertain strangers" is only one word in Greek, meaning generally "to exercise hospitality." It is the same word used in the other passages we have already considered. It is translated here as specifically referring to strangers because the apostle here emphasizes that the guests are not familiar—they might even be angels. Some people, simply because they had a love for strangers and a desire for hospitality, have been given the great privilege of entertaining the very angels of God. Had they not remembered this duty, and had they not seen the blessedness of this obligation, they would have missed the opportunity and all the blessings that attended it.

Some have entertained angels in the earthly sense, for the word *angel* means only "messenger," and this messenger may be human or spiritual. Rahab entertained the spies sent out by Joshua, the widow at Zarephath entertained Elijah, and the woman at Shunem showed hospitality to Elisha. All of these women were entertaining angels—the human messengers and servants of God. Others have actually entertained supernatural messengers, that is, those we usually think of as "angels." Abraham ran to meet three strangers, not knowing that two of them were angels, and one of them was the Angel of the Lord—a theophany of the Lord Himself. After the two angels had left Abraham, Lot took them into his home in Sodom, and they in turn led his family out of the city before it was destroyed. The apostle in Hebrews reminds us that all of these saints took in angels unwittingly. They had no idea who the strangers were who turned up on their doorsteps, and that did not matter to them. They showed love to the stranger, without expecting anything in return, and were rewarded for it.

Everyone would like to have a famous or powerful person in their home, but it is not true hospitality to entertain someone because of their prestige, or ability to repay your trouble in some way. The apostle tells us to entertain strangers without regard to their identity. If they need help we should help them. Hospitality brings great blessing those who show it freely in this way. The main point is not to keep us on the lookout for angels. The main point is that we should be ready and faithful to show compassion and kindness to strangers, whoever they are, because it brings us unexpected blessings to do so. Recall the parable of the sheep and the goats, when Jesus says to the sheep, "Come, ye blessed of my Father, because I was a stranger and you took me in, I was naked and you clothed me, I was in prison and you came to visit me" (Mt. 25:34–36). The blessed ones are confused by this—"We didn't ever do those things for you, Jesus. What do you mean?" Jesus replies, "When you did it to one of the least of these my brethren, you did it to me." When someone welcomes a believer—no matter how seemingly weak, lowly, or dirty—he is actually welcoming Christ Himself. That is the point of entertaining strangers, when they are of the body of Christ. If I do not show love to His body, how can I say that I love Him? John Calvin once said, "If someone will object that entertaining angels is an unusual occurrence, I have a ready answer, in the fact that we receive not only angels, but Christ himself, when we receive the poor in his name. If we do it unto the least of His brethren we have done it unto him."

The love of the world is an abstraction, and one that is very easy to talk about. Anyone can say, "I love the poor," and most of them can even be sincere. But they mean that they love the poor whom they do not know. They love the poor across town, who will never come to their door. They love the poor whom they will never touch. We all know that our congressmen and senators "love" the disadvantaged, but have they ever met them or invited them into their homes? Only then would they understand how difficult it can often be to deal with different kinds of people, and how much they can try one's love. It is easy to love people with whom one has no contact, and the world is all too full of this abstract and worthless love. This love does not care to actually help others, aside from perhaps guiltily throwing a bit of money at them. The biblical love God commands is never a subjective emotion; it is always manifested physically, tangibly, and visibly. Hospitality is a concrete, down-to-earth test of our love for God and for his people. One can talk all he pleases about his concern for the weak, lonely, crippled, and difficult members of the body, but he does not love them until he has proved that concern with action.

The Elders and Hospitality

Timothy and Titus both contain a list of qualifications for those who wish to hold the office of elder. *All* of these qualifications are required for *all* elders; the test is pass/fail, and only a perfect score passes the test. This does not require sinlessness, but it does require significant fruit in every area listed. Paul gives Timothy the following requirements: "This is a faithful saying: if a man desires the position of a bishop [or elder], he desires a good work. A bishop must be blameless, the husband of one wife, temperate, soberminded, of good behavior, hospitable, apt to teach, not given to wine, not violent, not greedy for money..." (1 Tim. 3:1–3). Every elder must be hospitable, demonstrating an open, gracious heart.

Titus 1:7–8 contains a similar command: "A bishop must be blameless, as a steward of God, not self-willed, not quick tempered, not given to wine, not violent, not greedy for money, but hospitable." Here, hospitality is given in contrast to greed, hot temper, drunkenness, and violence. Being hospitable is the opposite of a number of vices, and so it drives them out. If one is hospitable, we know that this is consistent with being a lover of good things, soberminded, just, holy, and self-controlled. If one is not hospitable, any number of vices may be present, for inhospitableness is a form of selfishness, and selfishness tends to express itself in many ways.

The elders are the representative men of the congregation, and as such they must be what every member ought to be. Regardless of differences in gifts and calling, every Christian is called to pursue these qualities, and the elders are called to pursue them in order to provide an example for others. They are called to constantly remind the congregation of their responsibility to be generous and self-sacrificing.

The New Command

Our Savior told His disciples in the midst of a pagan culture that love was the one great commandment, a "new" commandment. He did not call it a new commandment because it had never been given before (Lev. 19:18), since even the scribes knew that it was the second greatest law. Rather, He called it new because by fulfilling the law it defines Christian ethics, and He wanted to emphasize it in a way that the disciples would never forget. He went on to say that love would be the distinguishing mark of His disciples in the world. It is the most important testimony in a pagan society that the church can give, able to attack and tear down all pagan strongholds. True disciples love each other and demonstrate that love in real, tangible ways; if we do not love one another, our profession of biblical theology is no different than a profession of the theology of Maharishi Mahesh Yogi, and the world will not discern anything distinctive or even attractive about us. But as a whole the church has failed in love, and this is precisely what has happened—Christianity has become just one more religious option among many. The individual in search of spirituality is told to go to an ethereal smorgasbord, and pick out whatever suits him.

Once, upon meeting a stranger, I asked him if he was a Christian. He said, "Well, yes—partly." I replied, "Which part?" (I assumed, however, that this "part" was not his head.) He identified a few aspects of Christianity that suited him, and then a some aspects of Buddhism and Eckankar that suited him better. He had chosen from the smorgasbord and was quite satisfied with himself, for by setting himself up as the judge of truth, he was really only a follower of one religion: the church of Self. He did not realize how the church of God stands against him and how utterly meaningless it is to detach one part of God's truth from another. No one can be a "part" Christian. Anyone baptized in the name of the Father, Son, and Holy Spirit, who is has not been lawfully excommunicated, *is* a Christian, and the only question is whether or not he is a consistent one. Many Christians today live with inconsistency, denying that the Scriptures have authority and making themselves the judges of God and truth. Only the sovereign grace of God can change and revive us. When it does, we shall relearn true love, and the world will be confronted with the realities of covenant community. Such a community, when it speaks an unapologetic declaration of the truth, is unanswerable. It is a necessary expression of consistent Christianity, and by God's grace will reverse the destructive trends in the modern world.

This community is founded on real and manifested love. One of the chief manifestations of love is the grace of hospitality. There are few things that are more commended to God's people, or commanded of them, than this grace. It is central to the well-being of the church and crucial for our testimony, particularly at this time in history. We need to rejuvenate and clarify our vision of the church and its mission to the world. Without biblical hospitality, we can never be what we are called to be—the covenant community of God's people—and so we will be unable to perform the collective duties God has given us. Hospitality is like the mortar that holds bricks together. It matters little if we have deep and rigorous theological knowledge, but do not have this; for then we are nothing but an inconsistent and impotent church.

Hospitality is one form of love in action. It is not a matter of indifference to us, and it is not something to leave to happenstance. Paul exhorts us to excel in it, to chase and pursue it. We do not dread it as a grievous burden, but glory in it as the privilege of encouraging and building up God's people. Peter exhorts us to practice it without grumbling. Why should we grumble? It is essential for the well-being of the church, and it brings great blessing to those who pursue it. We should rather embrace it gladly, remembering that some have entertained angels unawares. Hospitality is the open, free, natural expression of covenant communion with Christ. We who have received so freely from Him, now gladly and freely give to others. What will this mean? We must turn from any selfish concerns for privacy, convenience, a leisurely schedule, an immaculate house, or any other excuse. There are things many times more important: the glory of God and the good of His people.

Chapter 7
The Nature of Hospitality

Many of us who are older recall times when these were ordinary and expected virtues that could be observed in nearly the entire country—at least, outside of the large cities, which seem to have difficulties with them in every age. We once expected kind, Christian treatment as a matter of course, and we usually got it; we would have been shocked *not* to receive it. Today, the world is very different, and whenever someone happens to receive kindness from a stranger, he is amazed and writes a letter to the local newspaper, to tell everyone how wonderful it was actually to meet a considerate and truthful person.

This is a symptom of cultural disintegration, and if we as Christians fail to understand and apply the commands of hospitality in the covenant community, our churches, like our culture, will eventually die. As the Christian memory is lost and as respect for Christian moral standards erodes, we will continue to see, with increasing starkness, what we have witnessed the last twenty-five to thirty years. Having seen the scriptural commands in the last chapter, I'd now like to discuss the characteristics of hospitality.

In a world like ours, anyone who wishes to talk about hospitality will probably sound rather outdated and obsolete, as if he wants to return to *The Little House on the Prairie* or perhaps Mayberry. We do not have time for that sort of thing—too many important things to do. Who can be hospitable in the realities of our 24/7 world? I wish that such thoughts only entered the minds of unbelievers, but it is evident that the vast majority of churchgoers think in the same way because the surrounding culture has so successfully infected us with their philosophy of time. One of the most common complaints against churches is that they are unfriendly, and it is the most common complaint because it is true. We have lost the sense and the spirit of the Scriptures on this topic. The problem can be traced back to the simple neglect of hospitality. God's people have drifted away from what the Bible teaches and what God expects of them in this area. Many of the woes of the modern church can be traced to a neglect of this most holy privilege and obligation. For we truly have neglected it. Hospitality, where it still exists, is largely an unstudied virtue. It springs from the particular personality of individuals or the circumstances in which they are placed, but it is not done as a matter of principled obedience, as it should be. Regardless of personality, circumstances, wealth, or social standing, this is an obligation that requires discipline and diligence, like any other difficult part of the Christian life. God commands it of us for our good, for the edification of the church, and for His own glory, and it is slack carelessness to leave it to happenstance or convenience.

Loving Strangers

The word for *hospitality* in the New Testament actually means "love to strangers." To be hospitable is, by definition, to be a stranger-lover. Obviously, *a fortiori,* we are hospitable to our friends and family, but the word refers especially to those outside that circle. The condition of strangers in the ancient world is one reason for this emphasis. Strangers were mostly ethnic foreigners, and most cultures of the world viewed them as enemies. A stranger was a threat; he had no protection under the law, and he had no legal rights. Far from being tolerant and cosmopolitan societies, the Ancient pagan cultures were hopelessly provincial. Noncitizens were usually far below citizens on the social scale. The stranger was a threat to the community, entirely at its mercy and as such could be treated with impunity. Most of us know the story of Lot helping the two strange men who came to Sodom (Gen. 19:1–11). Lot was streetwise, and he quickly invited them into his house to spend the night. They responded, apparently being very naive, that they were content to stay in the street, but Lot knew the inevitable result of that course of action and practically ordered them into his house. Even as it was, the citizens attempted gang rape and murder and were only stopped by a miracle. That is one example of the quality ancient pagan hospitality.

Israel was, therefore, quite unique in the world, because God commanded them to treat strangers kindly. "You shall neither mistreat a stranger nor oppress him, for you were strangers in the land of Egypt" (Exod. 22:21). "And you shall not oppress a stranger, for you know the heart of a stranger, because you were strangers in the land of Egypt" (Exod. 23:9). "The stranger who dwells among you shall be to you as one born among you, and you shall love him as yourself, for you were strangers in the land of Egypt. I am the Lord your God" (Lev. 19:34). With these laws, God set Israel apart from the nations of the world. His people would show kindness to strangers in order to show forth His grace to sinners. All men are strangers to God, being born far away from Him and cut off in their sins. God treats strangers with grace, mercy, and longsuffering, and expected His people to do the same, thus revealing Himself in their daily actions.

We are not, however, to take the command of hospitality as a mechanical absolute, for certainly there were limits to the reception of strangers. For example, they could not be criminals or lawless men. If they were unbelievers living in Israel, they were to submit to its laws and not practice immorality or seduce Israel to idolatry. No one is obligated to welcome a lawbreaker or dangerous man, thereby endangering himself and his family. We are not directed to exercise hospitality indiscriminately to anyone who might appear on our doorstep. If someone came by your house and wanted some food, it is not necessarily a good idea, particularly in this day and age, to let them inside, sit them down at your table, feed them, making yourself completely vulnerable to them. In our culture that is a risk, and the command does not require it. We usually find in the Scriptures that the stranger referred to in the command is a believer or at least a God-fearer of some kind. Christ uses the word *stranger* in this way in the parable of the sheep and goats. He welcomes the sheep because they ministered to Him by ministering to His brethren. "Assuredly, I say to you, inasmuch as you did it to one of the least of these My brethren, you did it to Me" (Mt. 25:40). It is clear that the sheep are commended for kindnesses to strangers *who are Christ's brethren*, that is, they are also the brethren of His people. The church has always understood hospitality in this way—directed to fellow believers who are unknown to us. The *Didache*, an ancient book of practical Christian instruction that was written in the first or early second century, teaches Christians to receive any stranger who comes in the name of the Lord (*Didache* 11:4–5). It goes on to say that if he stays longer than three days, he is a false prophet—in other words, if he keeps hanging about and taking up space, kick him out. Anyone who professes Christ was to be treated as an object of care, but there were safeguards against suave hypocrites and lazy men who would exploit the generosity of the saints. The main point is that we should not refuse hospitality to someone just because he is unfamiliar to us; we should take his confession seriously until he proves it otherwise.

We can define hospitality, then, as the art of receiving and ministering to strangers by showing biblical love to them. Our love ministers to others in a very real, practical, and powerful way, and it is even able to alter their position within the community. But what does that mean? What is the true nature of biblical hospitality? Clearly, it is *not* what we might call "entertaining." We often think that we play the host only for the purpose of amusing our guests. We feel the need to put on a show, go here, go there, watch this, listen to that, and do something else. People then become afraid to invite others into their home because they do not want the pressure of entertaining them. They feel that they need to keep everyone singing and laughing and talking for an entire evening, and many people just do not have that gift. Fortunately for our sake, the biblical burden is much lighter and within everyone's grasp. Hospitality is not fulfilled by entertaining others, but rather ministering to them, serving them, and meeting their needs. Our object is not to overwhelm our guests with the magnificent food or the brilliant fun they are having or to impress them with some self-glorifying show, but rather our object is simply humble, sacrificial service designed to encourage, build up, bless, and refresh them. You need not be a showman or have a gaudy stage to do this.

People avoid true hospitality because they have a false and exaggerated idea of what it is. When hospitality is considered to be a show, excuses to avoid putting it on come easily. "My house is just a mess, and it is not much of a house to begin with." "I'm not a chef, and can't make fancy meals." What do those things have to do with hospitality? The concept has been radically misunderstood. Those who think this way are coveting slick magazine ideals of home life. They are thinking of cocktail parties to impress bosses. That is *not* hospitality. Hospitality is humble, sacrificial, and imparts blessing and refreshment. It is not a means to build up our reputations or meet our own social needs. There are some people who have great personal and psychological needs that they meet by constantly bringing others into their home. Such behavior is selfish, draining and using other people, getting instead of giving. C.S. Lewis once pointed out the kind of woman who "lives for others; you can recognize the others by their hunted look." She wanted to live for others, but her "love" only resulted in further estrangement. We must avoid this kind of false hospitableness, which seeks to only to satisfy itself. We need to build up the church and not ourselves.

Hospitality As God's Graciousness

Hospitality is based upon three things. The first is the gracious nature of God. He is a God who is good to strangers because of this we are obliged to do the same. Our hospitality is rooted in His goodness and grace. We are by nature strangers, cut off from Him because of our sins, helpless to provide for ourselves, and He separated us for Himself, initiated a saving relationship, and clothed, fed, protected, and housed us. His people are thus commanded to follow His example and show hospitality to those who have no friends. Notice how God identifies Himself and Israel, and His application of these facts, in Deuteronomy 10:17–19: "for the Lord your God is God of gods and Lord of lords, the great God, mighty and awesome, who shows no partiality nor takes a bribe. He administers justice for the fatherless and the widow, and loves the stranger, giving him food and clothing. Therefore love the stranger, for you were strangers in the land of Egypt." Every time God commands His people to love strangers, He tells them the reason: they themselves were in the same position once. They were once strangers, and they received grace and hospitality from Him and even from others. The Lord is the generous God who gives to all men graciously; He is host to the world. As Paul points out in Acts, God has always made a witness for Himself, in the rain from heaven and the fruitful seasons, and in filling our hearts with food and gladness. Now *that* is hospitality. "Blessed be the Lord, who daily loads us with benefits, the God of our salvation!" (Ps. 68:19).

Now we, who have received His gracious benefits and His provisions, should also follow His example. Paul tells the Galatians: "Therefore, as we have opportunity, let us do good to all, especially those of the household of faith" (Gal. 6:10). Throughout the Bible, God's people are always very conspicuously hospitable people. In Genesis 18, Abraham lifts up his eyes and sees three men standing afar off. He immediately runs to them and asks them to stay and eat. Lot, knowing the dangers of Sodom, when he sees the two angels come into the public square (but before he knows they are angels), insists that they come to his house. In Job 31:32, Job vindicates his character with this statement: "No sojourner had to lodge in the street, for I opened my doors to the traveler." No one ever had to sleep on the street if Job knew about it. Peter stayed with Simon the tanner whenever he went to Joppa (Acts 9:43). Simon's house became Peter's home away from home, and his headquarters for spreading the gospel. He was staying there when he received the vision of the sheet, and when the three men from Cornelius come to him, Simon invites them to stay the night at his house as well, before they take Peter back with them. Luke records in Acts 28:7 that when they arrived in Malta, "there was an estate of the leading citizen, whose name was Publius, who received us and entertained us courteously for three days." In Romans 16:23, Paul mentions another man who understood hospitality: "Gaius, my host and the host of the whole church, greets you"—Gaius must have been quite a hospitable fellow to host an entire church. As we saw above, John commended another Gaius in 3 John 5:8, who had also been famously hospitable to the brethren. Again Paul tells Timothy of his good and loyal friend Onesiphorus: "The Lord grant mercy to the household of Onesiphorus for he has often refreshed me and was not ashamed of my chain" (2 Tim. 1:16). Philemon was so hospitable to Paul, that Paul was confident to say, "Meanwhile also prepare a guestroom for me, for I trust through your prayers I will be granted to you" (Phm. 22). I think we would all be glad to have a friend like Philemon, whose house was always open to the saints.

In Scripture, it is a common occurrence that when men are converted, they immediately begin to extend hospitality. Jesus saw Zacchaeus, the chief tax collector who had climbed a tree trying to catch a glimpse of Him, and He said, "Zacchaeus, make haste and come down, for today I have to stay at your house" (Lk. 19:1–10). Zacchaeus obeyed and received Him joyfully in his house. Lydia, when the Lord opened her heart to believe the things spoken by Paul, made a similar show of love. "And when she and her household were baptized, she begged us, saying, 'If you have judged me to be faithful to the Lord, come into my house and stay.' And so she persuaded us" (Acts 16:15). The apostles could not refuse these first signs of Christian love. Lydia had to show forth something of the grace that she had received, by ministering to those whom God had used to bring her to life. Clearly, one of the foremost manifestations of God's grace in the hearts of His people is their great desire to show hospitality. All who receive the grace of God are provoked by the Spirit of God to follow His gracious example.

Hospitality As Covenant Union

Just as there is a real union between each believer and God, by virtue of covenant, so there is a real union between each believer and all others. We often mistakenly think of the church as a kind of bottle, filled up with a loose collection of marbles, and its only purpose is to hold these distinct, atomized individuals together in one location for one day out of the week. They are together, but there is no real bond between them. This is far from the truth—in that we are joined to Christ, we are joined to one another as well. We are members of one another and cannot exist in isolation from each other. Covenant community is not a nice fringe benefit of Christianity; it is essential. A Christian cannot exist apart from it, and those who are isolated are in great danger of perishing spiritually. No individual member can prosper apart from the whole. Our American mentality of individualism and anti-covenantalism deludes us into thinking we can exist by ourselves—"just me and Jesus." On the contrary, if they actually listened to Jesus, and understood His role as the Head of a new race, He would tell them that they need both Him and the church, His body. He saves men and women through the ministry of His body, and the metaphor of a body is not used lightly; it is full of instruction. If a person cut off his little finger, what happens to it? It does not find itself, or realize its dreams, or grow to be independent, mature, and strong. Disconnected from the nourishment of the body, it disintegrates ignominiously into nothing. A similar decomposition occurs when a believer is isolated from the body. He causes suffering to himself and to the body, because we need others in order to prosper in grace.

"Now indeed there are many members" (1 Cor. 12:20)—the covenant does not destroy our individuality, thanks be to God— we are all very different and I hope that we love that truth, laugh about it, and fully appreciate its consequences. I hope that all Christians can delight in the amazing beauty of the lawful variations that exist between us. "There are many members" and the covenant of God's grace does not destroy personality, but rather sanctifies it. Each member still remains himself, though it is always a better self when joined to the body.

Paul continues: "but there is only one body. And the eye cannot say to the hand, 'I have no need of you.' Nor again the head to the feet, 'I have no need of you.' No, much rather those members of the body which seem to be weaker are necessary, that there should be no schism in the body, but that the members should have the same care from one another." No matter how "honorable" or "dishonorable" a certain member may seem, all are necessary to all others, and no member can do anything of itself. We need each other. The unity of the body of Christ inspires a holy sentiment, but being theologically grounded; it is not mere sentimentalism. Our interdependence is natural and inescapable, because God uses the ministry of each individual member to sanctify and build up the whole. "From whom [that is, Christ] the whole body joined and knit together by what every joint supplies, according to the effective working by which every part does its share, causes growth of the body for the edifying of itself in love" (Eph. 4:16). Paul does not give us a picture of each member having a personal pipeline of grace from Christ, each drawing his nourishment directly from Him. Rather, the picture is of Christ as the head; he energizes, strengthens, and blesses the whole body. His blessing is mediated through each of the members to each of the others. He does minister to individuals immediately by His Spirit, but He normally builds us in grace by our interaction with the other members of the body. No one can grow in grace without the body. It is impossible to grow up in fullness of maturity apart from its ministry. Thus fellowship and hospitality is one expression of our necessary and vital fellowship with one another. Hospitality is founded upon the covenant union that exists between God's people. We are one body.

Hospitality As Brotherly Love

The third pillar of hospitality is the mutual love that God's people have for one another, for it is one of love's primary expressions. In the New Testament, the commands to perform this duty always occur in the context of our larger duty of love. "Let brotherly love continue. Do not forget to entertain strangers, for by so doing some have unwittingly entertained angels" (Heb. 13:1–2). Hospitality is a mark of thriving brotherly love. Peter says, expecting the end of the age, "therefore be serious and watchful in your prayers. And above all things have fervent love for one another, for 'love will cover a multitude of sins'" (1 Pet. 4:7–8). Love covers sins, because its fruit is to take away the things that divide believers. Its manifestation, Peter explains in the next verse, is this: "Be hospitable to one another without grumbling." In Romans 12, Paul gives various commands, beginning by charging us to be living sacrifices to God. In verse nine he says, "Let love be without hypocrisy.... Be kindly affectionate to one another, with brotherly love in honor giving preference to one another, not lagging in diligence, fervent in spirit, serving the Lord, rejoicing in hope, patient in tribulation, continuing steadfastly in prayer, distributing to the necessities of the saints, given to hospitality." Hospitality is one of the clear manifestations of biblical love and affection. When believers love each other with sincere hearts, they will sincerely pursue hospitality with all their heart. When a church does not delight in hospitality, it is the symptom of a fearful cancer in their midst, which will draw all vigor and the blessing from that body. Their love for Christ and His people has grown cold. For wherever there is fervent love for Christ, there is always fervent love for His people.

Beloved, let us love one another, for love is of God; and everyone who loves is born of God and knows God. He who does not love does not know God, for God is love. In this the love of God was manifested toward us, that God has sent His only begotten Son into the world, that we might live through Him. In this is love, not that we loved God, but that He loved us and sent His Son to be the propitiation for our sins. Beloved, if God so loved us, we also ought to love one another. (1 Jn. 4:7–11)

A loving spirit does not expect to be loved in return. Sometimes we think a loving person is a soul hungry for love, who is very sensitive to any slight, feeling sorry for himself and remembering every small offense which shows that people do not respect and adore him as he deserves. That kind of person does not have a loving or sensitive soul, but a simple and selfish one. A truly loving spirit responds to the love of God by brimming with love for those around him, and it is irrelevant whether that love is returned. He has been captured by the love of God and the profound depth of His response overshadows and annuls all other responses. He wants to love the brethren even if they do not love him. John continues:

No one has seen God at any time. If we love one another, God abides in us, and His love has been perfected in us. By this we know that we abide in Him, and He in us, because He has given us of His Spirit. And we have seen and testify that the Father has sent the Son as Savior of the world. Whoever confesses that Jesus is the Son of God, God abides in him, and he in God. And we have known and believed the love that God has for us. God is love, and he who abides in love abides in God, and God in him. Love has been perfected among us in this: that we may have boldness in the day of judgment; because as He is, so are we in this world. There is no fear in love; but perfect love casts out fear, because fear involves torment. But he who fears has not been made perfect in love. We love Him because He first loved us. If someone says, "I love God," and hates his brother, he is a liar; for he who does not love his brother whom he has seen, how can he love God whom he has not seen? And this commandment we have from Him: that he who loves God must love his brother also. (1 Jn. 4:12–21)

There are no alternative options here; the true lover of God loves the fellow saints. When we grow in this love, God extends more blessing to us. If we do not love each other, we may be sure that the Spirit is not dwelling in us. This love is one of the preeminent marks that distinguishes God's people from the world. In the above passage, John has expounded our Savior's words: "A new commandment I give to you, that you love one another; as I have loved you, that you also love one another. By this all will know that you are My disciples, if you have love for one another." (Jn. 13:34–35). Love distinguishes believers because the unbeliever is basically incapable of loving anyone but himself; selfishness, unconcern and indifference are the things that characterize him. His chief desire is to preserve his own peace and quiet and not be put out or inconvenienced by anyone else. But when a man is saved, his heart is changed from one that worships itself and its own convenience into one that worships God, and loves Him and His children. Because of this, the absence of hospitality is a fearful thing. If there is no concern for hospitality, there is no love for God's people. When there is no love for God's people, there is no love for Him.

We know very little about heaven and the eternal, glorified state, and when the Scripture speaks of it we should pay close attention. It is no accident that one of the more prominent images of heaven is a gathering and *sitting down* with Abraham, Isaac and Jacob (Mt. 8:11). If someone is not familiar with biblical hospitality, this cannot be much of a metaphor for future bliss. If we have no knowledge of biblical hospitality, we might be tempted to think, "So, we sit down...and then what?" Why doesn't this description ring with glory in our ears? Because we have never sat down at a table and known the joy of its fullness. Not a fullness of food, but of fellowship, a table where the saints sit, rest, talk, and enjoy the weight of God's goodness. In eternity we are freed to enjoy His goodness to our utmost capacity, together with Abraham, Isaac, Jacob and all kinds of strange and interesting people from all the corners of the earth. Our hope for heaven is dimmed by our failures to love on earth. The picture does not move us because there is no love for it to move.

Christ used this feasting picture in his teachings, but we find the same images in the Old Testament as well.

> And on this mountain, the Lord of hosts will make for all people a feast of choice pieces, a feast of wines on the lees, fat things full of marrow, of well refined wines on the lees. And He will destroy on this mountain the surface of the covering cast over all people, and the veil that is spread over all nations. He will swallow up death forever, and the Lord will wipe away tears from all faces. The rebuke of His people He will take away from all the earth, for the Lord has spoken. (Is. 25:6–8)

God wants us to know that communion with Him is to be desired more than the finest feasts and luxuries we now know. Thoughts of heaven should make one's mouth water. The feast of God is the most earnest desire of every true believer, and the worst punishment possible for a believer is cut him off from this table. The exercise of excommunication is a solemn but necessary duty; it always protects the feast, and hopes that the apostate will be stunned into repentance by his lost blessing. We must separate from him in the Lord's supper and in our own suppers. Paul commands, "I have written to you not to keep company with anyone named a brother, who is sexually immoral, or covetous, or an idolater, or a reviler, or a drunkard, or an extortioner. Do not even eat with such a person" (1 Cor. 5:11). Feasting together is the greatest privilege and ultimate goal of the Christian life; it is the best of earth and the foundation of heaven. Those who isolate themselves from it through sin and apostasy, who refuse to be hospitable and refuse the hospitality of others, including the ultimate hospitality of God, will receive exactly what they desire—separation from God, His people, and their table.

Chapter 8
The Benefits of Hospitality

Even in an age when, supposedly, federal law is breaking down all social barriers and inequalities, our personal and social relationships are in a worse condition than they have ever been. We no longer "bear each other's burdens" because we do not know or care about others' burdens. In such times it is more important than ever to demonstrate biblical love, a love based self-consciously on the covenant. When we discipline ourselves in this love, and especially in the love of hospitality, we will begin to see its many glorious consequences being worked out in our midst.

Thus far I have considered the foundation and nature of hospitality. It is the ministry of encouragement and help to others; its foundation is the grace of God, the covenant of His people, and the mutual love we have for one another. In this chapter I will consider the great benefits that accrue from cultivating the virtue of hospitality and these can be broadly organized under three headings, as they apply to the individual, the family, and the church of Christ in general.

Benefits To Individuals

Some of these benefits showed up in the broader discussion of friendship, but it's important to grasp the multifaceted nature of these central virtues. All these issues are interlaced, and we need to see them from many angles. For individuals, hospitality is a means of grace, by which we are sanctified, growing in the knowledge of Christ. Hospitality teaches us to esteem and care for others, and thus it teaches us to die to ourselves. Dying to oneself is a summary of the whole process of sanctification; we die to self so that we can live to God, to His people, and to His glory. "Let each of you look out not only for his own interest, but also for the interest of others" (Phil. 2:4). Hospitality gives the opportunity to think of the interest of others who are outside of ourselves, our own circles, and our own families. The exercise of hospitality focuses our attention on the struggles, needs, joys, and blessings of other people. We listen to their problems and solutions, victories and defeats, warnings and encouragements, and so are enabled to share in their lives. This is biblical hospitality because it meets the needs of others. Some people use hospitality for their own selfish reasons, but this is not true hospitality; this is using others to satisfy the self. Hospitality ministers to others and therefore helps people to forget themselves, to everyone's profit. It helps us die to ourselves so that we may minister to others.

Hospitality also teaches us how to be friendly. When confronted with the "duty" of friendship, most people react in one of two ways. First, they might reply, "I don't need to learn that; I'm a naturally friendly person. That is the way I am." Another would say, "I'm not a friendly person, and everyone else needs to learn to deal with it. I don't care. That's the way I am. Live with it." Both of these attitudes are wrong. No one is truly friendly by nature, because everyone by nature is a sinner, and sinners are not friendly people. Sinners have mixed motives even in their friendships. There is always a basic self-centeredness in sin, a desire to go in one's own way, and an assumption that one's whole life revolves around the self. Anyone with that attitude is not truly friendly. The other kind of person, who refuses to be friendly, is only expressing basic selfishness in a different way. Often these people refuse to reach out in friendship, but then expect others to attend to them and help them, and are frustrated in their self-imposed loneliness. Recall the proverb: "He who desires friends must show himself friendly." This seems to be common sense, but it is incredible how many people do not grasp it. They complain of having no friends, not realizing that their own selfishness is the problem. They show hospitality to no one, and expect everyone to show it to them. They believe that their church is full of exclusive cliques, and that no one cares about them, but they never stop to ask *why* no one seems to care—no one wants to associate with a self-consumed and self-pitying person. We would all do better to stop worrying about receiving invitations, and start worrying about *giving* them. Do not complain that others are not friendly to you; be friendly yourself.

If you demonstrate the grace of hospitality, you will never have to worry about having friends. Hospitality gives you the opportunity to grow in the grace of sanctification and learn the basic tools of friendship: patience, forbearance, love, sacrifice, kindness, forgiveness, and humility. No one can learn these virtues unless he practices them, and the practice of them requires constant contact with other people. Most people are very patient when they are alone with themselves. When someone is alone he does everything his own way, and has no need to accommodate anyone else. It is with other people that we find our character tested. Real patience, forbearance, love, kindness, forgiveness and humility can only be learned by living with sinners. For this reason Paul often talks about biblical love in negative terms, as in "Love is not easily provoked." He assumes that the saints' love has the opportunity to be provoked. Close community puts believers into situations that test them, and only then can their characters be exercised and strengthened. Hospitality gives us an occasion to grow in the tools and virtues of friendship.

Hospitality also teaches generosity. We are further sanctified when we learn to give of our time, talents, and resources for the benefit of others. We learn to prove the truthfulness of our Lord's teaching that Paul handed down to the elders of Ephesus: "It is more blessed to give than receive" (Acts 20:35). Part of the great joy of having blessings from God is the ability to share those things with other people. That is the only joy of possession. Where is the fun of having possessions if you are the only one who enjoys them? It is exciting at first but soon becomes a bore. The pleasure of having things lies in the giving of them to others. Jesus gives this as the only reason to desire material wealth. Why should we desire more money? So that we can have more to give. Giving is better. People who have very little, and give greatly from what they have, are far happier than those with great wealth who give little. Even if they only have a pot of soup to eat, and a small room to sit down in, they will want others to come and share the meal with them. They have learned the great lesson, that it is more blessed to give than to receive. Hospitality is the perfect way to experience the joy of giving. It leaves no room for the natural selfishness that suppresses all joy. The miser enjoys nothing. He has a great pile of gold to sit on, but gold is never comfortable as furniture. Comfort, rest, and delight are known only by the one who understands the generosity taught by hospitality.

Benefits To Families

The benefits extend to the whole family, and especially to the children. They can learn by example and imitation the things we should all know: generosity, friendliness, and selflessness. It is vital, not only that we learn these things, but that we raise up the next generation in them as well. They should grow up willing and able to be self-forgetful and openhearted. If they do not, our culture is as good as dead. This culture is already being destroyed and eaten alive by the radical selfishness of practical atheism. If believers now do not raise their children to have big hearts and open hands, the community will not survive. It will continue to exist—of course it will not crumble to dust—but it will exist only as a preserved corpse exists. It will go on, but it will be dead and cold.

So we need a generation that knows how to serve, and is

delighted to do so. How and where will they learn this? Will they learn it by listening to a sermon, or by reading this book? Should we send them to classes or conferences? We can do all these things, but should always remember that the home is the greatest classroom. Without clear examples of love, grace, and selflessness in the home, no amount of reading or lecture will help. The virtues of hospitality and friendship are not *taught*, but *caught*. Many sincere and godly Christians believe that a conference, a set of tapes, a book, or a lecture can solve everything, even if their homes are dead. Children do not learn things from books or sermons if the things are not confirmed at home. God ordained the real, practical teaching of parents in the family covenant, and it remains the most effective. If the home is not obedient, a hundred lectures will do nothing but confirm the hypocrisy. Real open hearts and doors are easily and joyfully imitated in action. The continual exercise of disciplined and glad hospitality is the best way to teach it to your children.

Because hospitality both teaches and gives pleasure, it will provide many holy memories to children. Children should remember more about their youth than just holidays, vacations, and the things they received for Christmas or birthdays. They should grow with traditions and memories that actually mold their perspective and stand out to guide their future lives. One of my memories of home is of my father always saying, "Never run out of food in front of guests." He would be upset if the bowl was close to being empty, because it seemed to tell the guests to hold back. I've always remembered that, and it still bothers me if any platters of food are cleared while we have guests to dinner. My father's point was that your overflowing abundance is a way of showing your guests that you want them to enjoy themselves. We had plain, simple food but we always had plenty of it.

Thousands of little experiences like this, when taken together, have an enormous effect on our children's thinking. They will grow up with a complex and intuitive knowledge of generosity and friendship. They should have memories of cheery Sabbaths, memories of sharing food and conversation with hundreds of saints throughout the years. They should know that the Lord's day is the great weekly day of celebration. Experiences like this change lives, and indeed will change the entire culture, when they are remembered and recalled as a model for the future. When your children think back on their childhood, they should want their household to be as godly. This familial obedience and celebration will change the world, not lectures or conferences or even sermons. These things will change the world, but they cannot be taught. They must be shown, exemplified, and demonstrated.

When the children see these examples, they not only learn obedience but also the pleasures of God's covenant. The unbeliever likes to think that unbelievers have all the fun, and that believers are fools for submitting themselves to the ethical standards of the faith. But he is wrong. Joyful Christians laugh at the suggestion that the unbeliever's licentiousness yields in any way a true and lasting happiness, but sadly many Christians fail to give, in their home life, a living refutation of the unbeliever; our lives have failed to publish the joy of the gospel. Our houses should be a place of celebration. Obviously it has limits; Paul warns believers not to fall into greed, lusts, and the revels of pagans. But the home is to have a spirit of godly and temperate celebration. In the home God's grace is celebrated every day and every week, but especially on the Lord's Day, through fellowship and godly conduct.

The idea of "keeping the Sabbath" does not have very positive connotations in our time, but this is because we have never seen the Sabbath kept in the way that God tells us to keep it. We rebel against the idea because we have an image of stern, Pharisaical people dressed in black, telling us in a severe tone that we can't do anything enjoyable, but must sit down all day watching the walls. That is what the Lord means, they think, when he commands us to "celebrate" the Sabbath. They have missed the whole point: when He tells us to *celebrate* the Sabbath, He means it; the Sabbath was made for us, not the other way around. God wants us to worship

Him and enjoy ourselves on His day. It is a day of rest and satisfaction, not boredom and idleness. Again, this does not mean that every Lord's Day should be a colossal party, or that having a day of quiet with the family is illegitimate or unholy. It is perfectly right to have times of peace and quiet with family, especially on the Lord's Day. The point is that every day—but particularly on this Day—our children should experience visible, tangible examples of the inexpressible joy that Christ grants His people, a joy that is founded on worship and the service of our fellow-saints. This is not to locate all joy in externals. Certainly there is great inward joy in knowing that Christ has saved us, and that His grace and its effects belong to us. But we cannot see inside each other, and most importantly, our children cannot see inside us. They need to see that joy expressed, and to experience it firsthand for themselves. Hospitality is one way in which we can show the joys of the covenant in this way.

Another benefit of hospitality to children is that they have the opportunity to learn from others. We who love covenant and family sometimes forget that the influence of godly people from outside the family is very important to the family. Because of this we hold conferences and invite people from around the country whom we do not normally have an opportunity to hear. In my experience, it has always been helpful to hear someone from outside my own circle, who has a refreshing and challenging perspective on different issues. Through these guests we can see how God is working in other places, reminding us of our connections with the larger church and with our common history. In short, it is a great blessing to have other Christians in one's house.

Visiting Christians strengthen our children by reinforcing the same things that their parents have been teaching them. Whether we like to admit it or not, outside verification is important to children, especially if they perceive their parents to be a bit eccentric in some ways! The children learn that their parents are not alone in their convictions, because they come to know many good people who believe the same things. It is good for them to realize that there are others who are zealous for the glory of God, and that there are some who love and serve Him in far more amazing ways than they have even seen before. Hospitality in this way is a great means of grace to children as they learn the ways of God from many examples, and they are stirred to holiness by the words and actions of the faithful guests who share the table with them.

Benefits To The Church

The blessing of hospitality does not stop at the individual and the family, but is poured out upon the entire church as well. The Scriptures constantly and implicitly assume that God's people will be often interacting together—not occasionally, not only once a week, but continually. Christians call themselves a people, an identifiable group, a community and household of faith. Those terms imply plenty of interaction, not only on Sundays but throughout the week. For this reason the epistles are always admonishing believers to be patient, to bear with one another in love, to forgive one another, to be kind, to give preference to one another, and so on. Why would they need these exhortations if they only see each other on Sunday for two hours? Most people do not need any great patience, forbearance, or humility to put up with others for two hours a week. But they do need these virtues badly if they are to be often in other's company, because everyone is a sinner and so has problems and temptations of some kind. Something in each of us will rub someone else the wrong way, and if we interact with people then we will come to know these faults, and we will learn the virtues that overcome them. If we refuse to interact with others, we will learn neither our faults nor our virtues. So many dead churches believe themselves to be unified and full of love for the brethren, but that is only because they never see each other. It is easy to "love," in a vague, abstract kind of way, someone you do not know. It is easy to be at peace with humanity in general, as long as you never have to reconcile with a real person. There is peace and unity in a graveyard;

there are no arguments and no divisions. But that is not the peace of the living; it is the emptiness of the dead. In a real, living church, growing under the blessing of God, members are rubbing shoulders constantly, and so there are constant outbreaks of conflict that require forgiveness, forbearance, and patience—growth in sanctification becomes a necessity; it is sink or swim. Such tensions are not necessarily a sign of immaturity. That is how large groups of sinners behave, and Paul assumes this situation and prescribes group virtues. Even though hospitality is only directly commanded a handful of times in the New Testament, it is always assumed, and it is impossible to exercise many New Testament virtues apart from it. It is not something peripheral or secondary, but central to a living, breathing, growing, functioning, vital, and blessed Church.

What are the particular blessings that comes to a church from the practice of hospitality? It is, first, a great encouragement to others, and so fulfills part of the requirement of love which commands us to provoke one another to love and good works. "And let us consider one another in order to stir up love and good works" (Heb. 10:24). The word *consider* implies the need to give careful thought and planning to this encouragement. What is the first thing the apostle mentions to help us accomplish it? "Not forsaking the assembling of ourselves together, as is the manner of some, but exhorting one another, and so much the more as you see the Day approaching" (v. 25–26). Of course the primary concern of the passage is public worship. But it also applies in a more general way: God's people need to gather together for mutual encouragement, and we encourage one another by visible manifestations of our mutual love.

It is not enough to have unity of spirit; that unity must be openly and visibly manifested. We are not disembodied spirits. It is disturbing when people try to strip away all adornments and get at some abstract, ascetic essence of living: "We don't need art or pretty music in our homes; we just need to read the Bible." Of course we read Scripture in our homes, but how can anyone think that beautiful music, art, or storytelling adds nothing, or even detracts from, the life of the home? The modern church does not understand these things because it is full of closet evangelical Gnostics, who think that physical things are not important as long as the mind is full of correct attitudes. But God commands open and manifested love. According to James, unless we show our faith by works, that "faith" is worthless. Holy affection for one another is to be openly demonstrated, and hospitality is one of the ways in which that is done.

The members of the New Testament Church were often together, and the unbelievers noticed this immediately. The unbelievers knew little or nothing about Christian theology, but they did see the love that was manifested; in spite of slanders that were circulating about the Christian community, they had to admit that the Christians loved one another. It was obvious to the world, whether or not they heard lectures or sermons on Christianity or the nature of love. In a modern world where there is so little holy love and affection, and where those virtues have been replaced by violence and lust, we must shine like those early Christians did in the Roman Empire, encouraging one another to hold fast in an unbelieving world. We shine and are strengthened through our mutual hospitality.

Using the Lord's Day for hospitality is especially appropriate in regard to encouraging one another. We have a chance to discuss the sermon, to grow in our understanding of it and its application to our own lives, learning the lessons of obedience from each other as we talk. We see and hear how others are working through the Word, trying to live faithfully. When we talk in this way it is, as the proverb says, like iron sharpening iron. We grow in wisdom and discernment, and our understanding of the Word takes on an edge it never had before. We better discern righteousness from error. We can derive great comfort from this mutual application of sound doctrine. Paul says, "Now, therefore, comfort one another with these words" (1 Thes. 4:18). He also says in 2 Corinthians, "Blessed be the God and Father of our Lord Jesus Christ, the Father of mercies and God of all comfort, who comforts us in all our tribulation, that we may be able to comfort those who are in any trouble, with the comfort with which we ourselves are comforted by God" (1:3–4). When we apply God's Word to ourselves, we are then able to apply it to others in the same situation. Godly fellowship is of incalculable value to growth.

The hospitality of encouraging words does not always have to be serious or lofty in order to be edifying. We should rejoice in the opportunity to gather and simply laugh with each other. This is not just a luxury, but an indispensable part of our fellowship. "A feast is made for laughter" (Eccl. 10:19). Laughter is not a nice extra at the feast; it is what the feast is *made* for. It is not a waste of time to sit at table, telling jokes and stories. Unfortunately some Christians think that the only profitable and edifying speech is talk about the Bible and theology, and that reading a funny story is a waste of time—especially on the Lord's Day! Where on earth do we get this idea? It is not only unChristian, it is inhuman. It is certainly not biblical; feasts are made for laughter. Failure to understand this is a failure to understand basic Christianity and what it means to glorify God. He expects us to laugh at ourselves and the world. If we are able to laugh, we have a proper perspective about ourselves, and we understand that God is in control of the world and He is working out His purposes. If someone cannot laugh, and thinks it is never profitable to read a funny story or to hear a good joke, then he is only showing that he does not understand the sovereignty of God. He is taking the world far too seriously, and above all things he takes himself too seriously. There is nothing holy or intellectual about such an attitude, and we should refuse to fall into that kind of spirit. There is too much of it in the world already.

Hospitality fosters an increase of love in the church. It both expresses and promotes greater love. It provides us with deeper knowledge of one another, and from that knowledge comes deeper and more sincere love. The more time people spend together, the more they learn about each other's lives, with all their trials, joys, struggles and sorrows, and knowing this leads us to love and sympathize more wisely. For this reason we are especially enjoined to show hospitality to strangers, so that we can know them and turn them into friends, so that we may know and love them better. We are enabled to meet and know others whom we would not normally associate with, whether because of divergent interests, occupation, or personality. We do not naturally choose to spend time with those sorts of people, and so we should make a special effort to fellowship with them. Otherwise, various groups and cliques begin to form and harden, becoming at best indifferent to each other, and at worst in conflict. People start to make judgments about the "strange ideas" that those "other people" have, taking every opportunity (clothing, inside jokes, interests, etc.) to distinguish themselves. Churches that do not have a full and deep interaction begin to fragment along these petty divisions because they promote mistrust and suspicion. But the free and wide exercise of hospitality can stop such destructive trends and establish harmony and loyalty in the body.

A third blessing to the church is that of evangelism. We should never underestimate the power of the fellowship table as a pulpit and strong witness to the world. I recommend that everyone read Martin Luther's *Table Talk* for perfect examples of this fact. Every day, Luther would have some group of people around his table, and he would talk to them about Christian thought and life. He would say some surprising and outrageous things, but also said many great things, and people often took notes of these informal sermons. Such teaching in the context of fellowship has an enormous impact on people. The table is a pulpit and the home is an evangelistic garden, and they teach in subtle and powerful ways.

Chapter 9
Stepping Toward Hospitality

Hospitality is not only a great privilege and blessing of the covenant that God has established among His people. It is an actual picture and metaphor of God's grace to sinners. We who were cut off, strangers from God, alone and without hope in the world, isolated in our sins, have been graciously taken into His household, and He has given us all that we need for life and godliness. He constantly feeds, nurtures, blesses, encourages, rebukes, and chastens us—that is what it means to be in God's household, receiving the fullest and most gracious hospitality of all. The salvation that God grants His people is the root of all the hospitality that they express to one another and to the world. The more clearly we understand His grace, the more obvious the privilege and duty of hospitality is, because in it we proclaim again the story of His mercy toward us. For this reason we are commanded to exert hospitality gladly, without grudging, complaining, or feeling imposed upon. It is a great honor to serve the Lord's people in this way, but that does not mean it is optional.

Food At The Center

As noted earlier, the Bible often tells us that the godly concern of a true friend is better than a feast. "Better is a dinner of herbs where love is, than a fatted calf with hatred" (Prov. 15:17). A bowl of turnip greens can be better than veal. The hungry soul, in a context of biblical love, is fed more by less. The starving soul is of first importance, and the actual food is secondary. If I can only afford crackers and peanut butter (to cite a fairly extreme case!), that is fine if I have it with love, fellowship, help, and encouragement. Again, "Better is a dry morsel with quietness, than a house full of feasting with strife" (Prov. 17:1). A house full of feasting cannot compare to a crust eaten with biblical contentment and love. Kindness satisfies in ways that the grandest meals and the most lavish arrangements cannot. Most people doubt whether they are able to be hospitable, because they do not have much to share with strangers. But regardless of how much or how little they have, it is love and kindness that drives hospitality. The Hebrews, for example, had already lost nearly everything. The apostle writes in chapter ten, "You had compassion on me in my chains, and joyfully accepted the plundering of your goods" (Heb. 10:34). Then in the very next chapter he reminds them to show hospitality. They have already suffered the loss of all things, but they still have the obligation of hospitality. If those who are truly destitute can exercise it gladly, then surely modern Americans can.

Having said all of this, it is important to balance our perspective, and clarify that even if something is of secondary importance, that does not mean it is of small importance. By emphasizing love and kindness, we should not at all belittle the significance of great food, feasting, and table fellowship. The Church, in the last hundred and fifty or two hundred years, has forgotten and lost much of her knowledge of feasting, which is quite incredible since table fellowship is highly significant in redemptive history. The first requirement of God's covenant, the duty that first kept man in communion with Him, centered around eating. Adam could eat from all the trees in Eden except for one. There was abundance, variety, and freedom within the limits of obedience and trust, and he could only break the covenant by eating the wrong food. Therefore the sharing of food, from the beginning, has been a sign of the covenant that exists between God and the sinners He has chosen for Himself. God eats with those whom He saves. The Lord, with two of His angels, was willing to eat with Abraham because he was a friend of God (Gen. 18). The Passover meal showed the terrible blessing of redemption and judgment. At Sinai, after God had given the law to Moses, He called Moses and the elders of Israel up to the mountain to eat and drink in His presence (Exod. 24). They shared a table with God, signifying the good bond of the covenant between them. In the wilderness God gave manna from heaven and water from the rock, both of which, we are told later, are signs of His presence and blessing to His people. For the yearly feast of tabernacles, the people laid aside a tithe of their income, and could spend it for whatever they desired as long as they ate and drank it in God's presence (Deut. 14:22ff). He merely wanted to see them enjoying His gifts—that was the only requirement. We tend to belittle "Israel under Law" as quite severe and miserable, but do any of our modern churches have such a celebratory tithe as this?

God's willingness to eat with us signifies His love, mercy, and His covenant union with us. This indicates that food is central to the purposes of God. We all know that it is necessary for sustaining physical life, but God has told us clearly that the meaning of food is much larger. We are commanded as God's people to take dominion over the earth, to serve the Lord, and by His authority to see the whole earth bring glory to Him, in every area of life. But development in all areas of life—arts, business, science, medicine, technology, or theology—is impossible if we spend most of our time hunting and gathering food. In societies like that, there is no great architecture, art, music, science, or literature. There is no time for it. Hungry people do not write symphonies. Therefore food, in a very obvious but important sense, is central to cultivating the world for the glory of God. The abundance of food makes dominion labor possible, and so food is one of the central blessings (or curses) of the covenant. If men rebel, God says that He will send them famine. When men repent, turn to Christ, and are restored to covenant communion again, the rain comes in its season and the harvest is full and blessed. They then have an abundance of food and can devote their energies to dominion labor. In Deuteronomy 28, this is the most prominent covenant blessing. When God promises to bring His people into the promised land, He describes it as a land of *food*. It is a land flowing with milk and honey and other tasty (and high-calorie!) fare—there are no "diet plans" in Canaan.

The Law was designed to convey to the people all the blessings of the new land, stipulating feasts that sometimes went for fully fourteen days. This astounds the modern mind. We have no clue how to do something even remotely like that. We cannot conceive of taking that much time off from work (except for our private vacations), and even if we did, we would be utterly unable to plan for such a celebration. We have become a culture ignorant of celebration and feasting. We think it is a waste of time and resources, because we have forgotten the historic knowledge of fullness of the gospel and the abundance of grace.

Try for a moment to imagine the status of Israel in the ancient world. In a world where famine was commonplace, God commands His people to have regular feasts every year. All around them people are starving because God has given them judgmental famines, and yet He tells Israel to have several feasts, each of which lasts at least a week. Today, we would not think that this is a very "fair" arrangement. Feeling guilty at our own prosperity and great use of resources, we would suggest sending all that extra food to the surrounding pagan nations who were less fortunate. But we fail to understand God's purposes in Israel. He wanted to show the world that if a people serves idols, they starve. If they repent and come back to the living God, they will have an abundance. God testified to this every year before the whole world, so that the world's jealousy would be provoked. They too would want a god like Him—a god who fed them and did not feed on them.

Thus, for redeemed man, feasting is a symbol and celebration of blessing and victory. "All the days of the afflicted are evil, but he that is of a merry heart hath a continual feast" (Prov. 15:15). The man who has the merry heart—a heart blessed by God—has a continual feast. His life is full of joy, so he sets aside times to properly and fully express that joy. Christendom has always made a point of having feasts throughout the year, so that we will not forget the great abundance of God's blessing on us. Consider the significance of the familiar psalm:

> Yea, though I walk through the valley of the shadow of death,
> I will fear no evil;
> For You are with me;
> Your rod and Your staff, they comfort me.
> You prepare a table before me in the presence of my enemies;
> You anoint my head with oil;
> My cup runs over. (Ps. 23:4–5)

The psalmist uses concrete things to express the blessedness of serving Jehovah. Even when he is hounded by enemies who are trying to devour him, the Lord spreads a table for him. We also can sit down in peace, even surrounded by enemies, because our confidence is not in our armament, or strategy, or unholy alliances with ungodly nations; our confidence is in God and therefore we eat with Him in their presence. We have such confidence in God's real presence that even danger does not damage our appetites. God's protection, partisanship, and provision are not just words to David, but very real things, upon which we can base our feasting. He says elsewhere, "The Lord is on my side, I will not fear; what can man do to me?" (Ps. 118:6).

The child of God can eat, drink, and be merry regardless of the consequences; he has a reason to give thanks because he alone has a true and irrefutable reason to eat, drink, and be merry. When the writer of Ecclesiastes says this, he is not giving an endorsement to orgies, as some unbelievers interpret it. He tells us to be *merry,* not blind drunk. "Nothing is better for man than he should eat and drink, and that his soul should enjoy good in his labor. This also I saw was from the hand of God" (Eccl. 2:24). This is not the language of a reveler; good things are "from the hand of God." Again, "I know there is nothing better for them than to rejoice and do good in their lives, and also that every man should eat and drink and enjoy the good of his labor; it is the gift of God" (3:12–13). "It is good and fitting for one to eat and drink, and to enjoy the good of all his labor in which he toils under the sun, all the days of his life which God gives him, for it is his heritage" (5:18). "Go, eat your bread with joy, and drink your wine with a merry heart, for God has already accepted your works" (9:7). God has accepted us; there is no reason to be distressed, or worried sick, or not to rejoice. Regular feasting, as a sign of God's great blessing to us in the covenant, is entirely appropriate for the faithful.

We need not be stingy with our provisions, having confidence that God did not lie when He promised to provide all our needs for all our days. This confidence gives God's people a freedom to be generous. Those who do not have this confidence are always afraid that what they have is not enough, and so are always seeking to gain more, because at any time it could all disappear in the blink of an eye. But the godly man, even if he has very little, always understands that when he obeys God, works hard, uses his gifts well, follows his calling faithfully, he need not worry about lacking necessities. He does not need to be afraid of generosity, because his confidence is not in possessions or savings accounts. Confidence is in the Lord, who promises that He will provide for all our needs. Thus grace produces a spirit of holy extravagance in the hearts of God's people. It is not wastefulness, but rather an unworried, unhampered generosity of spirit, which allows them to give to others even if they do not have much themselves.

We should be like the woman who brought to Jesus an alabaster jar filled with expensive and fragrant oil. She broke the jar and poured out the oil on his feet. The straitlaced disciples could not believe it (Mt. 26:6ff). "Do you realize how much money that is? We could have sold it and given the money to the poor." But what did

Jesus say? "Let her alone, you crowd of self-righteous conservatives. What she has done is good. She understands grace, and you do not, and because she understands, she can be extravagant. What she has done will be spoken of throughout history to her honor." There is no room for pietistic self-righteousness here. Feasting is one of the great marks of the fullness of God's blessing upon His people, and it is something extravagant and "unnecessary." But we desperately need to learn again how to do such "unnecessary" things (especially in our hospitality), and perhaps we will begin to learn what the truly important things are.

Joints and Fractures

Once we understand the important position food has in the Bible, we still need to know how to incorporate it into the practice of hospitality. No list of guidelines will encourage us on to real hospitality as much just jumping in and doing it. But the following suggests a framework for practicing hospitality. And finally, I'll discuss the enemies of hospitality—those things that weaken the structure. My thanks again to Alexander Strauch for starting me thinking down this path.

As we saw earlier from the meaning of *pursue*, it is not enough for someone to agree in principle that he has some responsibility to be hospitable. It is not enough to be willing to extend hospitality if someone asks you to do so. It is not enough to be open to it if it is needed. We are to actively seek opportunities to exercise hospitality, pursuing it, chasing it down, running hard after it. Passivity in this area is simply disobedience; aggressiveness is necessary. You do not need a large home, or a great deal of money, or any special skills as a chef. All you need is a willingness to spend time and effort on practicing and developing a hospitable mindset. The one important thing to remember is that this is not optional, no matter what excuses one might invent to put it off. Lack of time, money, or space is not the issue. We are to pursue hospitality with the resources we have, and to seek to broaden those resources so that we may pursue it more and more.

Hospitality requires *planning*. If you do not plan for guests, the chances are that you will not have any. It is all too easy to miss the many opportunities for hospitality because of this. Anticipate occasions where you know you might have a chance to invite someone over, and be ready to do so on fairly short notice. The Lord's Day is one obvious time to plan for hospitality. It is full of opportunities. Plan for it unless you have good reasons not to—and there will sometimes be good reasons to refrain, such as sickness in the family or a lack of sleep because of an especially hectic week at work. There are many legitimate times to refrain, and we would miss the entire point if we tried to force obedience in an unrealistic, rigid, or legalistic way. But the point is that the Lord's Day is a ready-made opportunity for opening our homes to others, whether they are visitors or members whom we do not yet know. Special events and conferences are also natural times to plan for hospitality. Finally, if any fellow believers are under any hard providences, that is one of the most obvious and important opportunities to minister to them in this way. We should never be caught off guard.

Isaiah, when describing a righteous people and their reign, describes them as *planners* of generosity. They are contrasted the ungenerous foolish and wicked, who plan evil; the foolish person "no longer will be called generous, and the miser will not be said to be bountiful" (32:5) even though he has wealth. He is not bountiful or blessed. "Also the schemes of the schemer are evil; he devises wicked plans to destroy the poor with lying words, even when the needy speaks justice. But a generous man devises generous things, and by generosity he shall stand." (v. 7–8). The wicked man spends his time plotting how to destroy the poor, but the good man spends the same effort devising, or "plotting," how to help them. The godly must spend time planning their generosity; it is not something to do off the cuff. We need to learn "holy scheming." Notice also that the virtue of the generous turns back into a blessing for him: "And by generosity he shall stand." Perhaps this is what Jesus meant when he said, in the parable of the cunning steward, "make friends for yourselves by unrighteous mammon, that when you fail, they may receive you into an everlasting home" (Lk. 16:9). The "mammon" refers to things that we do not worship but are still needful for life, such as food, clothes, money, and other forms of wealth. One reason God gives us these things is so that we can use them to make friends, who are able to repay our help in our time of need.

So we should always be ready to take advantage of opportunities to exercise hospitality. If we are to "entertain strangers," as the author of Hebrews says, we should be prepared for such unexpected guests. If we are ready, entertaining them is an opportunity of great pleasure instead of an occasion for panic. If we do not plan, difficulties and objections arise immediately in our minds, and it will be easy to let the chance slip by. Any duty that involves some difficulty or trouble will seem tedious unless we remember its beauty and usefulness, having already made the necessary preparations for it. Then, when the need arises, we are ready to fulfill our duty with joy and gladness.

Of course, there will be times when you are caught completely off guard, and someone needs your hospitality at the worst possible time. In such cases, we should remember a bit of wisdom that one woman I know gave to her daughter. Some people who needed hospitality had surprised the daughter at a bad time, and her house was in no fit state to receive them. So she suggested that everyone adjourn to the porch and spend the evening there. When her mother heard about it, she admonished her with a bit of excellent advice: "Never allow pride to get in the way of hospitality." Hospitality is always more important than impressing your friends with housekeeping skills. Plan for it under normal circumstances, and do not be stressed in abnormal circumstances. This does not imply that we go to the other extreme and not care what the house looks like when we have guests. To clean up before guests arrive is simple courtesy. I may be accustomed to having some degree of disorder; I may be used to stepping over the kids' various toys left around the living room. But guests should not have to do the same. The mess is my responsibility, not theirs. We should not expect them to put up with our laxity, so we should make things as neat and clean as possible for them. But we all know that there will be times when we are caught off guard, and have not had a chance to clean up. In such cases, graciously lay down all pride and never let it interfere with hospitality.

There are a number of specific aspects of planning for hospitality, but we do not have time to lay out and explain all of them. However, I do want to give a few practical tips to think about. First, make a list of people whom you need to spend time with. If you have not had the chance to get to know someone, add them to this list, and you will not forget them when it comes time to invite people into your home. Second, gather a collection of solid and inexpensive menus that can feed large groups of people. Third, keep a supply of "hospitality food" on hand—something cheap, edible and filling. Nothing fancy, of course—just something that is handy and ready in a moment's notice, so that you can be ready for any opportunity that presents itself. Obviously this kind of meal is not an epic feast, but remember that the ultimate goal of hospitality is not necessarily to impress people with expensive, gourmet food, but to minister to and serve them. The focus is on the open door, not the elaborate and full table. The purpose is not to entertain but to help, serve, and profit other people, so we must be aware of the importance of instruction, godly conversation, the pure, simple, enjoyment of one another. The open door signifies a willingness to minister to others, rather than always seeking to be ministered unto. The open door is a sign of the open heart, and the open heart is one that has been flooded with the love of Christ and the grace of God.

We must finally remember to *persevere* in hospitality, especially if we haven't had much practice doing it. Many modern

Christians have grown up in homes where it was not often practiced, and so it is understandably a daunting and frightening thing to get into. We have never seen good examples of it; we have little idea of what it is like, and we know that we will probably make a million mistakes. This is a real problem, but we ought not solve it by avoiding it. The solution is to face it head-on, and gradually we will be accustomed to it. If we do it long enough to become skilled and practiced in it, *then* we can start to enjoy it. When a child first learns to ride a bicycle, it is not a very enjoyable experience. It requires some work, discipline, and determination before any benefits are seen. The child is tense and rides carefully with a constant dread of falling and hurting himself. But he perseveres until he learns it deep down in his body, and can do it without conscious effort—only then is he able to enjoy it. We all have a similar experience in doing nearly everything that is worthwhile—whether it is reading, education, music, art, or, in this case, hospitality. Only perseverance and discipline produce the sort of easy skill that eventually widens not only our ability in it but our capacity for enjoying it.

Perseverance in hospitality makes it habitual, a natural, expected part of the weekly routine. Developing a hospitable mindset overcomes most of the difficulty of obedience in this area, and we develop this mindset through continued application. The practice of it should become a simple "given." It will become, not something special or extracurricular, but an integral part of the curriculum itself. When it becomes a part of this through extended discipline, even though it always will task us, it is no longer possible to think of it as a burden. It is, instead, an anticipated joy, the satisfaction of working at something and becoming proficient in it.

Crippling Selfishness

To help us exercise the positive virtue of hospitality, we need also to be aware of the various enemies and pitfalls that will destroy or distort it. The first enemy, of course, is *selfishness*, and it is an enemy that is ingrained in our very nature. We like to have everything conform to our own ways; we resent other people interfering with our desires, our stuff, our plans, and our peace. Because true hospitality disrupts this selfish desire to be left alone, we tend to react against it. But we must face the simple fact of obedience: Is personal peace and quiet more important than the good of God's people? We cannot ignore this question; it is the real crux of the issue. Sanctification is dying to oneself; unless *you* are willing to die to self, *we* will never be a hospitable people.

The prime example of selfishness—greed—especially destroys hospitality. We are unwilling to share what God has given to us, because everyone's portion seems small in his own eyes. In a more subtle way, we think that in times of scarceness we should be excused from exercising hospitality. But that is not the nature of Christian duty. That is not what Peter wrote to his persecuted and embattled audience, when he urged them to become *more* hospitable. Generosity is not fulfilled if one only gives those things he does not need or cannot himself use. If he is only sharing from his superabundance, he does not understand grace. That is the attitude of the wealthy Pharisee, measuring out his tithe in spoons, while the poor widow next to him gives her last two pennies. True grace and generosity is like God's: we who deserve nothing have been given everything *richly* to enjoy, and Christ paid a heavy price to give it to us. Out of this reality grows a sense of true gratitude that enables us to give gladly from what God has graciously supplied to us. The same gratitude prompted the Macedonians to a remarkable generosity: "in a great trial of affliction the abundance of their joy and their deep poverty abounded in the riches of their liberality..." (2 Cor. 8:2). God showed them the beauty of His work and His grace to them, instilling such deep joy that in adversity and poverty they *abounded*. No one needed to ask them (few would have the nerve, considering their condition); instead, they did it voluntarily in an overflow of joy.

The whole point of generosity is that we gladly give from whatever supply we have, so that others might enjoy with us the things we have been given. That is the whole pleasure, beauty, and blessing of it. In that act we show that we do not put trust in our possessions, but in the God who gave them—there is an immense difference between the two, and we manifest that distinction in our generosity. We believe that as He supplied them in the past, He will supply them in the present and future. We let go of worry. Generosity overcomes anxiety. Generosity therefore is a powerful testimony to the grace and generosity of God, a testimony which we sorely need today. But greed of any kind, even if "excused" by a felt lack of sufficient resources, destroys hospitality and destroys this testimony. We are to give voluntarily from an abundance of joy, and from what we have—not what we believe we need.

A Disorderly, Undisciplined Lifestyle

If our lives, homes, and routines are in a state of disarray, and we are hardly able to sufficiently take care of ourselves, we will naturally be discouraged from ministering to others. The house may be unkempt or the children disorderly; there may be no peace, respect, or honor shown in the family. There is no godliness or enjoyment there and instead it is full of strife. People who live like this avoid having guests because they know that a house of feasting, yet full of strife, is worse than no feast, and no one wants to be there.

But the true answer to this problem is not to avoid hospitality, but to repent and deal with the sin. If there is no love between husband and wife, he must ask forgiveness and start loving her, seriously and sacrificially. If children are disorderly, discipline them and teach them how to act like Christian human beings. Teach them respect. Do not tolerate whining and complaining. The Scriptures teach that part of a loving parent-child relationship involves the rod. Discipline, applied consistently from love and not from anger, is a beautiful and not a cruel thing. Children respond to it wonderfully, and when they come to maturity, reaping some of the "peaceable fruit of righteousness" (Heb. 12:11), they thank and bless their parents for it.

If your house is not a haven for your own family, how could other people possibly enjoy being there? The home life should address the family before anyone else. It should be a refuge for them. The children should want to be there. Does your child not like to stay at home? Why? If they are always wanting to be elsewhere, that is a symptom of the strife and lack of joy in the home. Something is wrong with the home, and it requires repentance and obedience. If your house is not a haven to your children, it will not be a haven to other people. If your house is not a haven to you yourself, why do you want to invite people there? Just to aggravate them so that they can have a taste of what your unhappy life is like? Hospitality in an unhappy home makes no sense whatsoever. It begins with loving the members of your own household, and making your house into a gardenlike place of peace, rest, and refreshment. When it is cultivated in this way for you, it will then also be a place of refreshment and rest to others. A lack of discipline is sometimes just an expression of lack of love. Some of us must face this—we simply do not care about others in the household of faith. Where there is no love, there will be no desire to serve them, encourage them, build them up, or stir them up to live faithfully. Without love, and the intimacy it involves, how can we care about their well-being, their burdens, or their needs? Without love, we don't even want to know. In this failure our radical individualism and lack of covenant awareness plays its biggest role. It becomes an unspoken, unconscious excuse for not exerting ourselves to minister to the needs of others. Where there is no love, there will be no hospitality.

Lack Of Love For Christ

The final enemy of hospitality is ultimately a lack of love for Christ himself. Hospitality flows from our deep gratitude to Christ. Those who are willing to be hospitable have learned that the true marvel of the faith is not that people are able to love one another; it is not even that people are often able to show love to strangers. The ultimate marvel is that God loves people. He knew them inside and out, in all their wickedness, inconsistency, hypocrisy, deceitfulness, violence, cruelty, pettiness, and ugliness, and yet He loved them. That is the central miracle. When that fact is grasped, hospitality, being rooted in it, grows and flourishes. The more we contemplate this first Love, the more we begin to understand what it means to love each other. Hospitality flows from the recognition that all we have has come to us by the gracious hospitality of God. Our acts of hospitality are merely the faintest reflections of our gratitude to Him for His great love to us. That is why the Savior said that on the last day, He cannot recognize those who do not show love to strangers in His name (Matt. 25:31ff). Christ is united with His people, in that they are His body. If someone refuses to minister even to the least of its members, he insults Christ directly. "Inasmuch as you did not do it to one of the least of these, you did not do it to me."

In a world that is becoming more consistent with unbelief, few things will become more strange than the practice of hospitality, of kindness to those who have no claim upon others apart from faith in the same Lord or from suffering brought on by the sin in the world. The love of Christ enables us to minister sacrificially to strangers outside our own circles of family and friends. Remembering that He took us in when we were strangers, we also continue to extend love to the strangers we meet and because of His love and mercy we can do this with unrestrained joy. No one can ever be hurt by generous hospitality. In giving of ourselves and our resources, our time, money, and labor, we can be assured we will not be hurt, nor will we "lose" anything. Just the reverse: we shall receive more than we have given. "He who sows sparingly will reap also sparingly. But he who sows bountifully will reap also bountifully" (2 Cor. 9:6). God is able to make all grace abound to His people. He is able to give us seed for sowing, that we may reap bountifully. Remember the words of Jesus: "Give, and it will be given to you: good measure, pressed down, shaken together, and running over will be put into your bosom. For with the same measure that you use, it will be measured back to you" (Lk. 6:38).

The great poverty of the modern church is not a financial poverty. We have plenty of money, always enough and often even more than we need. Our poverty is a poverty of spirit, a close-hearted, closefisted, narrowness of spirit that is utterly unChristian. It is another perverted Puritanism which is a complete distortion of true, healthy Puritanism. Distorted Puritanism worries over its joys, and spends more time feeling guilty over its blessings than it does enjoying those blessings. That is most emphatically not Christianity. The early Protestants were accused by the papists of having a faith that was "too glad to be true," as C. S. Lewis once said. The Protestants could not possibly have had the truth because they were *too happy*. They laughed and enjoyed life—and that, according to the Catholics, simply could not be biblical. I dare say that there is not one unbeliever in a hundred—or perhaps a thousand—who would accuse the church of this today. The church today has a rather negative image; it is fixated on sin, or it negates life, or it is full of petty moralists. To our great shame, unbelievers never accuse us of being too happy to have a true faith. But that is exactly the heart of Christianity that the world needs to see. Full-blooded, vital, undiluted Christianity rings in the ears of small, shriveled souls as a message to glad to be true. The rose of the gospel is so sweet and lovely that they cannot but suspect a poisonous thorn somewhere behind it. But we need to show them that it is as glad as it sounds and gladder yet than that. We show it, not primarily in our sermons, but in our lives. We have to eat, drink, and be merry in order to preach the full gospel. This is the motto of biblical Christianity in a world of vanity, which the wise man of Ecclesiastes said long ago: "Go, eat your bread with joy, and drink your wine with a merry heart; for God has already accepted your works" (Eccl. 9:7)